HORACE WALPOLE'S MEMOIRS

Horace Walpole's Memoirs

by

GERRIT P. JUDD, IV

BOOKMAN ASSOCIATES
New York

For

Lewis Perry Curtis

Preface

THIS ESSAY PRESENTS an analysis and evaluation of Horace Walpole's memoirs, which enjoy continuing popularity as a standard source of English history in the eighteenth century. It is based on my doctoral dissertation submitted to Yale University in 1947. In returning to it after twelve years, I have added some new materials from recently published works, notably Butterfield's *George III and the Historians*. But I have found little reason to revise the main conclusions, which are here presented for the most part as they were originally written.

I am deeply indebted to Wilmarth S. Lewis, editor of the monumental Yale edition of Walpole's correspondence, who graciously made available to me his unique Walpole collection. Warren Smith and George Lam, staff editors of the Yale edition, gave freely of their time and knowledge. Professor Lewis Curtis directed my dissertation with insight and forbearance. A small token of my regard for him appears in the dedication. Finally, I am grateful to Hofstra College for a grant which made possible the publication of this book.

Contents

ERRATA

Page 47, line 11—*for* to *read* is

Page 65, line 2—*for* prevent *read* present

Page 72, line 29—*for* digusts *read* disgusts

Page 85, line 26—*for* inventive *read* invective

Contents

1.

··

The Composition of the Memoirs

HORACE WALPOLE's memoirs and journals extend over a period of 45 years. As early as 1746 he was writing his "Memoires, from the Declaration of the War with Spain," a brief work never published.[1] Five years later he began his *Memoirs of the Reign of King George the Second*, which, although originally intended to cover only one year, extend from 1751 to the death of George II in 1760. His *Memoirs of the Reign of King George the Third*, begun in 1766, carry the narrative from the accession of George III to the death of the Princess Dowager in 1772.[2] *Last Journals* start where the memoirs leave off and end in September, 1783, and the unpublished "Journal 1783–91,"[3] a fragmentary work, completes the series.

The manuscripts of the memoirs were preserved with other papers in a box, delivered, according to the provisions of a memorandum which Walpole left among his effects, to John, sixth Earl Waldegrave, on his reaching the age of twenty five.[4] Walpole left specific instructions about the contents of the box. "When you shall have time," he wrote, "to read over the mass of papers contained in this box, you will find that they are not proper to be seen by anybody at present; and therefore I trust that you will not mention the contents to anybody, but reserve them in your custody. They are most imperfect both at the beginning and end; nor do I wish *ever* to have them published; but as they contain a great deal of curious matter, you may like to have them preserved in your family."[5] Nevertheless Lord Waldegrave entrusted the manuscript volumes entitled Mem-

11

oires to Lord Holland, who edited for publication in 1822 the volumes on the reign of George II.[6] Lord Holland explained his action at some length. "Though no directions were left by Lord Orford [Horace Walpole] for the publication of these memoirs, there can be little doubt of his intention that they should one day or other be communicated to the world. Innumerable passages in the memoirs show they were written for the public. The precautions of the author to preserve them for a certain number of years from inspection, are a proof, not of his intention that they should remain always in the private hands of his family, but of his fears lest, if divulged, they might be published prematurely; and the term fixed for the opening of the chest seems to mark the distance of time when he thought they might be made public without impropriety."[7] At Lord Holland's death it was discovered that he had not undertaken the task of editing the remaining memoirs. They were accordingly placed in the hands of Denis le Marchant, who published in 1845 the *Memoirs of the Reign of King George the Third.*[8] In 1859 Walpole's *Last Journals* appeared, edited by Dr. John Doran.[9]

Extensive as they are, the memoirs form only a part of a much grander literary conception. Walpole deliberately set out to record the history of his own time, not only the political events but all aspects of English life. He once remarked, "Mr. Bentley says that if all antiquarians were like me, there would be no such thing as an antiquarian, for I set down everything for posterity so circumstantially, that I leave them nothing to find out."[10] One critic has called him the greatest social historian of his time.[11]

The reason Walpole undertook this monumental task is not far to seek. His friend Gilly Williams once remarked that Walpole's wish to be remembered by posterity "has been his whole aim. For this he has wrote, printed and built."[12] Walpole himself confirmed the general purport of Williams' observation when he stated that he had "always lived in terror of that oracular saying . . . 'the sons of heroes are loobies.'"[13] Ambition to be remembered in his own right as Horace Walpole, and not merely as a son of Sir Robert Walpole, the famous statesman, was the main emotional force behind his literary career.

In intellectual terms his wish "that posterity may know all about it"[14] originated largely in his realization, shared by Dr. Johnson, Chesterfield, and Voltaire,[15] that much history was imperfectly understood—an idea which may have come from his father.[16] In the preface to his *Historic Doubts on the Life and Reign of King Richard the Third* he stated, "All very ancient history, except that of the illuminated Jews, is a perfect fable. . . . If we take a survey of our own history, and examine it with attention, what an unsatisfactory picture does it present to us! How dry, how superficial, how void of information!"[17] Elsewhere he stated, "History is a romance that is believed; romance, a history that is not believed."[18] To Lady Ossory he wrote, "History, I believe, seldom contains much truth."[19] To Lord Hailes he exclaimed, "How seldom is history fairly stated!"[20] Walpole hoped that he might prevent the history of his own time from being as poorly understood as that of ages past.[21] In so doing he would indeed be remembered as more than a great man's son.

He began by collecting his materials. For his *Anecdotes of Painting* he bought the manuscripts of the engraver and antiquary George Vertue. He assembled and bound 59 volumes of tracts and pamphlets on the reign of George III, 59 volumes on the theater of George III, and 22 volumes of verse published in the same reign. His bound copies of the *London Chronicle* ran to 36 volumes. He owned a complete file of the *Gentleman's Magazine* 1731-95, 33 volumes of the *Annual Register,* and 28 volumes of the *European Magazine,* as well as a large number of tracts, plays, and newspapers, all in addition to an unusually rich library of more formal printed works. At Strawberry Hill, his Gothic country seat, Walpole also accumulated numerous portraits, drawings, and miniatures, coins and medals, rings, and miscellaneous antiquities. His collection contained materials of far greater value than the hat of Cardinal Wolsey and the spurs of William III which Macaulay singled out for ridicule.[22]

The next step was annotating and note taking. As he once remarked to Cole, "I am apt to scribble notes in the margins of all my books, that interest me at all."[23] Some of Walpole's annotations have been printed, such as his marginal comments on Pope's verse, Chesterfield's letters, Mason's satires, and the works of Sir Charles Hanbury Williams.[24] He also annotated many other books in his library, to say nothing of his collections of tracts and newspapers, which bear frequent witness to his devotion.[25] Unlike many annotations, Walpole's are often full and almost invariably as pungent and to the point as the footnotes which he wrote to his own letters and memoirs.

A few of Walpole's rough notes have been preserved. He had a habit of jotting down memoranda in a commonplace book, on the back of letters, or on any scrap of paper which came to hand.[26] He faithfully recorded the anecdotes told him by Lady Suffolk, and used them extensively in his memoirs and correspondence.[27] His Paris Journals for 1769 contain a series of brief jottings which he expanded in his memoirs.[28] Some of his notes appear in the memoirs themselves.[29] It is known that he took notes of the Parliamentary debates for later inclusion in the memoirs, and on at least one occasion (the debate of January 22, 1752) he sent a copy of his Parliamentary notes to the Duke of Bedford.[30] Otherwise he polished up his memoranda for his correspondence. How heavily he depended on them appears toward the end of the *Last Journals,* where he apologized for the scantiness of his narrative with the explanation that his notes for the period were either lost or imperfectly taken.[31]

It was only after his materials had been collected and annotated, and his notes arranged, that Walpole approached the third step in the creative process, that of writing. His works include political pamphlets, a history of English painting, a catalogue of royal and noble authors, an essay on gardening, and a number of miscellaneous works, such as his *Reminiscences* written for the Berry sisters.[32] All of these served in one way or another to elucidate the history of his own time.

Walpole's chief literary production was his correspondence. It was in his letters, even more than in his memoirs, that he wished to chronicle his period. He chose his correspondents with care. Horace Mann, the British minister at Florence, was in many respects the ideal person to receive what amounted to a monthly newsletter. Mann had entertained Walpole while he was in Florence on the grand tour; they had friends and tastes in common; and it was of professional interest to Mann, as a servant of the government, to be kept informed of political events which were often imperfectly reported in the newspapers. But Walpole's letters to Mann were by no means exclusively political. He usually devoted only a paragraph or two to politics, filling out the rest of the letter with news in general, gossip, anecdotes, and a few literary items. In consequence this 45-year correspondence presents a balanced picture of English life which is unsurpassed in the eighteenth century.

In his letters to George Montagu, Walpole concentrated on the social side of life. On one occasion he deliberately revealed his intention, "to show you the manners of the age, which are always as entertaining to a person fifty miles off, as to one born an hundred and fifty years after the time." [33] After his disagreement with Montagu in 1770, Walpole continued his social letters to Lady Ossory. Walpole's correspondence with Cole was mainly antiquarian, that with Mason mainly political and literary, that with Gray mainly literary. Thus, by selecting his correspondents shrewdly, Walpole was able to find expression for the many facets of his interests, in a literary medium where he was unexcelled.

Walpole turned to memoirs for a number of reasons. In writing letters he was constantly inhibited by the knowledge that they were liable to be opened at the post office—a common eighteenth-century complaint—and it was only when he sent his correspondence by a private hand that he could write freely.[34] He doubtless shared Swift's feelings, that "my letters would be good memoirs, if I durst venture to say a thousand things that pass; but I hear so much of letters opening at your post office, that I am fearful." [35] In writing memoirs, scrupulously concealed from all but his most intimate friends, Walpole was able to express himself without reservation. Consequently, during his lifetime the existence of the memoirs was a closely guarded secret. Gray knew about them, as did Montagu, who may have read parts of them, and it is possible that Mann knew of them as well.[36] But John Pinkerton, with whom Walpole was fairly intimate toward the end of his life, apparently did not suspect that they existed.[37]

Moreover, the memoir as a literary form reached the apex of its popularity in England during Walpole's lifetime, and degenerated thereafter. The art of memoir writing, as an "informal compound of history and autobiography," had first flourished in France during the sixteenth century, and became prominent in England about the time of Charles II's restoration in 1660, probably in some measure as a result of the continental influences to which his court had been exposed while in exile.[38] Bishop Burnet commented on the popularity of French memoirs in England in 1677, and himself wrote a mixture of history and memoirs, as did Clarendon.[39] But as the eighteenth century wore on, the memoir began to fall into some disrepute. Printers used the term to describe books which properly speaking were not memoirs at all, and the term soon became almost meaningless. Johnson's *Dictionary* (1755) contains as a secondary definition of memoir, "hint, notice, account of any thing." Besides, history, autobiography, biography, and the novel were quickly evolving as literary forms in their own right, and soon superseded the memoir, which had been a sort of amorphous prototype of each.[40] Yet in the years of Walpole's young manhood this specialization was far from complete, and the memoir was still a respectable and vigorous literary medium.

Walpole became interested in memoirs early in life. About 1740 he wrote in his commonplace book, "Memoirs are of two sorts, either of one's self or of another; the former are generally false, and the latter seldom true." On the next page he added, "Memoirs are a kind of old wives or Canterbury tales, as appears by the etymology of the word which comes from the French *memoire*, or *memory*; now old stories often begin with, *I remember to have heard such a one say*."[41] A few years later he returned to the subject and wrote, in a more mature vein, "I chose the word memoires, because having been used by men, who from their course of life and occupations, are not supposed to be tied down to correctness, it has been indulged a latitude, which is not pardoned in historians. The intention of this work being to let my readers rather into the character of the actors, than into the minute events of the drama."[42]

Memoirs appealed to Walpole because they were fashionable,

the pastime of a gentleman's leisure rather than the work of a professional writer. Walpole and his aristocratic contemporaries despised any literary work which involved pedantry.[43] With the "beautiful negligence of a gentleman" [44] Walpole deprecated the labors of the scholar. "I hold authors cheap enough: what merit is there in pains, and study, and application, compared with the extempore abilities of such men as Mr. Fox, Mr. Sheridan, or Mr. Pitt?" [45] He had at one time contemplated writing a History of Learning and a History of Humanity, the latter to cover the reigns of Nerva, Trajan, Hadrian, and the last two Antonines, but the hostile reception which his *Historic Doubts* met in the hands of the critics dissuaded him from such ambitious projects, even if he had ever seriously intended undertaking them in the first place.[46] Burnet, whose writings Walpole admired, had pointed out that memoirs were easier to write than history, for the memorialist need relate only those events with which he was familiar, while the historian should take a comprehensive view.[47] The Earl of Ailesbury had remarked of his own memoirs, "All this is very irregular, and would not be pardonable in one that would pass for an historian, but I disown that character." [48] The memoir as a literary form was particularly attractive to Walpole, not only because it was fashionable, but because it was flexible. He could hope to find free expression in it without submitting to academic restraints for which he was temperamentally not well suited. He believed besides that memoirs offered opportunity for a more flowing literary style than did a scholarly treatise.[49]

In a number of passages addressed to future generations of readers Walpole clearly stated his intentions in writing memoirs. He expressed the belief that they were an accurate and impartial narrative of the main political events of his own time. That posterity might be correctly informed about the politics and politicians of his era was his primary stated intention.[50] Walpole's secondary stated purpose was to portray the spirit of his age in a series of anecdotes and trivia not necessarily related to the more solemn procession of "historical" events, that is, to give "the minutiae of which I have observed posterity is ever most fond . . . the omissions that historians in their grandeur disdain to record, which the humble reader most painfully labors to recover." [51] In addition he expressed the hope that posterity might be amused with his memoirs as well as informed by them.[52]

Several aspects of Walpole's program invite comment. In the first place, his preoccupation with posterity was characteristic of his period. Becker has observed that in the eighteenth century "posterity, like nature, was often personified, reverently addressed as a divinity, and invoked in the accents of prayer." [53] The appeal to posterity had ample classical and Renaissance precedents. Tacitus and the fifteenth-century memoir writer La Marche had invoked the judgment of future readers, as did Clarendon, Cardinal de Retz, Lord Hervey, and Gibbon.[54]

Walpole's stated purpose is also interesting in that the emphasis centered on politics. Analysis of the contents of his memoirs and journals indicates that, unlike his correspondence, they are mainly concerned with such matters as Parliamentary proceedings (the reports of debates constituting almost one-quarter of the total material presented), government policy, elections, and changes of administration, together with anecdotal accounts of the intrigues and squabbles of politically prominent personages. In this respect he conformed to the main tendency of historical thinking in his age. Gibbon's remark, "Wars and the administration of public affairs are the principal subjects of history," is a representative dictum. Eighteenth-century historians as diverse as Archdeacon Coxe, Hume, and Robertson all tended to share Gibbon's view.[55]

At the same time Walpole's program is significant in that it included a tentative formulation of what has come to be known as social history. His statement mirrors the growing awareness of eighteenth-century historians that matters social as well as matters political deserve serious attention.[56] But, just as his contemporaries failed to conceive of social forces as an important determinant of history, so Walpole tended to include social materials in the memoirs somewhat apologetically, as a sort of comic relief to political events.

Walpole made it abundantly clear that he wished to write in a fashionable rather than a pedantic manner, and he was consequently careful to distinguish his memoirs from formally written history. "I am no historian," he declared, "I write casual memoirs; I draw characters; I preserve anecdotes, which my superiors, the historians of Britain, may enchase into their weighty annals, or pass over at their pleasure." [57] In a later passage he stated, "It must not be supposed that I would pass off these trifling anecdotes of myself and others for a history of England." [58] In the first place, as he pointed out, his memoirs were not comprehensive, since they left out much material to be found in the newspapers or in such obvious public records as the journals of the Houses of Parliament.[59] In this respect he echoed Burnet, who had declared, "My chief design in writing was to give a true view of men and of counsels, leaving public transactions to gazettes and the public historians of the times." [60] Following the same line of thought Lord Hervey wrote, "The things that might be commonly known, I shall conclude too are so . . . I shall give more of private transactions, and connect little incidents less likely to be inserted in all other records of this reign." [61] Walpole avoided detailing military events on the sound ground that he was unable to understand them, just as he avoided full discussion of legal and constitutional questions, matters of revenue and finance, Indian affairs, and in later years (when they were fully and accurately reported elsewhere) the Parliamentary debates.[62]

Walpole's second main distinction of his work from formal histories was that his memoirs lacked the consistent point of view which he associated with a finished work. He admitted freely that, written as they were over a long period of time, his memoirs reflected his many changes in attitude, and he anticipated the charge of inconsistency by pleading that his work might lose its freshness if he attempted too much revision. "I choose to leave it as I wrote it, having at each period spoken truth as it appeared to me. I might have made it more uniform by correction; but the natural coloring would have been lost." [63]

Walpole indicated thirdly that his memoirs contained much "unhistorical" material, such as the long accounts of minor political transactions in which he himself participated, the numerous anecdotes with which he enlivened his pages, and the

trivia of the social world which merely amused the reader or
lent color to the general narrative.[64] He would probably have
agreed with Charlotte Lennox's statement that "such little cir-
cumstances will, by some persons be judged beneath the gravity
of history; but certainly whatever unfolds and displays the
hearts of princes is worthy of an historian's pen."[65] In any case,
Walpole was unquestionably right in assuming that most historians in his time, Robertson in particular, would have condemned as undignified the inclusion of such matter in a formal
work.[66] Walpole expressed the wish that his memoirs be judged,
not as a comprehensive, polished, and unified treatise, but rather
as one document among the many which he anticipated would
descend to scholars interested in the political history of the
eighteenth century. His bequest to posterity was, as he saw it,
a narrative containing only the raw materials of history. "I
recommended to posterity," he wrote, "to use their own dis-
cernment, abandon the author, accept what truths he has
delivered, correct his mistakes, condemn his prejudices."[67] At
that time, "my narrative, that may serve for the scaffolding, may
be thrown by as no longer of use."[68]

Finally, Walpole protested repeatedly that he did not expect
posterity to be edified by his writings. "Few persons," he once
commented, "profit much from history."[69] To Lady Ossory he
wrote, "I observe that no improvements of science or knowledge
make the world a jot wiser."[70] On another occasion he commented to Lord Beauchamp, "The world is not easily cured of
prejudices, nor does it love truth, which I can honestly say has
always been in my view."[71] To Montagu he declared, "It is idle
to endeavor to cure the world of any folly, unless one could
cure it of being foolish."[72] On the other hand Walpole, like other
writers of the Enlightenment, lived in an atmosphere heavy with
moral values. In his memoirs and other writings he did not hesitate to make moral judgments. On occasion he expressed the
frankly didactic view, held by such men as Bolingbroke and
Chesterfield and so characteristic of eighteenth-century historical
thought, that history is philosophy teaching by example.[73] Speaking of the elder Pitt, he commented, "The lights and shades of
a great character are a moral lesson."[74] A little further along he

wrote, "I wish to warn posterity (however vain such zeal) against the folly and corruption and profligacy of the times I have lived in." [75] But in protesting that he had no wish to edify his readers Walpole was protesting too much. His often-repeated denial of a moral purpose in his memoirs was in fact a studied and transparent pose.

2.

···

Walpole's Philosophy of History

ALTHOUGH WALPOLE repeatedly distinguished his memoirs from formal historical works, his ideas about history largely determined the character and content of his memoirs, for, as he defined his terms, he believed his memoirs to be a sort of informal history. Because eighteenth-century works of history concentrated on political events, Walpole in his memoirs, as has been noted, placed his main emphasis on politics. Similarly his concept of the working of the historical process and his grasp of historical method are worth examining, because they formed the critical standards by which he selected his material and made his interpretations.

Walpole nowhere left a detailed statement of his conception of the historical process, but his point of view appears in his general approach in the memoirs and in a number of isolated statements to be found there and in his other writings. It is evident, to begin with, that—like most historians of his day[1]—he had little inkling of the importance of economic pressures, social conditioning, institutions, or ideas as historical determinants. He did not go beyond the proposition that history consists of a series of mechanical events caused by men. Therefore, he reasoned, in order to understand historical events one had only to acquire an intimate knowledge of the actions and personalities of the men involved in them. Otherwise, "posterity would see sudden and extraordinary changes, without being able to account for them from the public appearance of things." [2]

He may have received his view of history from his reading

of memoirs, for it has been suggested that "the memorialist was the first to sense the value of history in terms of personality." [3] In any event, Walpole believed that the effective cause of historical events lay in the conflict of personalities. Thus the opposition to the Excise Bill of 1733 was, as he interpreted it, really opposition to his father; the war with Spain was fomented, not on any broad principle, but in order to oust Sir Robert Walpole from the direction of the government; the Duke of Cumberland's unpopularity resulted, not from his own brutality, but from stories about him circulated by the Jacobites and the Prince of Wales; and Conyers Middleton's works were attacked, not on issues of theological disagreement, but from personal hostility to Middleton himself.[4] Invariably Walpole interpreted events in terms of men. Once he had isolated the human factor in the historical equation he did not look farther.

In the sameness of human nature Walpole saw the dominant unifying force in the historical process. While on the grand tour he wrote, "The farther I travel the less I wonder at anything: a few days reconcile me to a new spot, or an unseen custom; and men are so much the same everywhere, that one scarce perceives any change of situation. The same weaknesses, the same passions, that in England plunge men into elections, drinking, whoring, exist here." [5] Two hundred years before, Machiavelli had expressed an identical view.[6] In the eighteenth century Voltaire shared this concept of human nature, as did Hume, who stated, "Would you know the sentiments, inclinations, and course of life of the Greeks and Romans? Study well the temper and actions of the French and English . . . Mankind are so much the same, in all times and places, that history informs us of nothing new or strange in this particular." [7] While belief in the sameness of human nature was not universal in the eighteenth century, it was widespread.[8] For the most part Walpole and his contemporaries, ignoring other determinants, tended to conceive of the historical process as a "repeating decimal" in terms of unvarying human nature.[9] The twentieth-century view differs in two particulars: first, that many determinants, and not one, work to bring about change; and second, that human nature may be variable instead of constant.[10]

Walpole accepted a second widely held eighteenth-century concept, that "trifles gave birth to serious eras," and that the historian should "trace the stream of events to their secret source," in order to discover "the mysterious springs" behind the incident.[11] Much of his annoyance with medieval chroniclers, as expressed in the preface to his *Historic Doubts*, arose from their failure to uncover the "remoter springs of action" and the motives behind the overt events.[12] Cicero had expressed belief that small causes can produce great events, a view which appears in the memoirs of Cardinal de Retz, in Swift's writings, in Chesterfield's letters, and in Lord Hervey's memoirs.[13] Hume spoke of "secret causes"; Charlotte Lennox emphasized "secret intrigues;" and Wraxall mentioned the "secrets of affairs." [14] The notion was familiar in English folklore in the form of the proverb beginning, "For want of a nail the shoe was lost," and ending with the loss of the kingdom, while Bolingbroke and Voltaire gave it classic expression in their explanation that the real cause of the Treaty of Utrecht was a spilled glass of water.[15]

Acceptance of such a view of historical causation stemmed in part from the Englishman's curiosity to learn what went on "behind the scenes" in the government—an effective factor in the popularity of memoirs in the eighteenth century.[16] But fundamentally its acceptance proceeded from the widespread view of history as a series of mechanical events.[17] In the absence of such limiting determinants as institutions, economics, or ideas, it was comparatively easy to present a muddled chain of causation in the spirit of *post hoc, ergo propter hoc*. Croce has expressed the twentieth-century view of the matter, "that the explanation of a fact is always to be sought in the entire organism and not in a single part torn from other parts," and some modern historians have gone so far as to refuse to discuss events in terms of "causes." [18]

To a twentieth-century reader Walpole's explanations of events may appear superficial, and his memoirs may seem to contain much irrelevant matter, but viewed in the light of his concept of the historical process, with the typical eighteenth-century emphasis on personality and secret causes, his preoccupation with character analysis, gossip, and minor intrigue has a plausible *raison d'être*. If men caused events, it was wise to be familiar with the characters of the men involved in them, and if secret causes operated to produce large results, no detail in an event, however trivial, was superfluous.

With respect to historical method Walpole was well abreast of his times. The whole concept of the memoirs, as he stated it, reveals that he was aware of the value of documentary evidence in written history. At his insistence the Earl of Powis consented to allow the life of Herbert of Cherbury, hitherto unpublished, to be printed at Walpole's Strawberry Hill press.[19] In 1758 Walpole bought the manuscripts of George Vertue, which formed the basis for his *Anecdotes of Painting*.[20] He had a major part in the rescue of the Conway papers, which he found in a state of deplorable neglect at Lord Hertford's country seat.[21] Walpole's interest in historical documents appears further in his comments on the papers of James II, which he saw at the Scotch College in Paris; in his own use of them as source materials for his *Historic Doubts;* and in his considerable manuscript collections, some of which were originally in the library of Sir Julius Caesar and Henry IV of France, and some of which he inherited from Madame du Deffand.[22] Walpole's contemporaries were becoming increasingly conscious of the importance of historical documents. The period from 1660 to 1730 has been called "the golden age of English Medieval scholarship." [23] Antiquarians such as Spelman, Cotton, Rymer, Hearne, and Walpole's friend Cole were active in preserving and publishing the records of the past, and Burnet in his memoirs had placed particular emphasis on documents.[24]

Walpole was also aware of the theoretical principles of handling evidence. In a number of passages he assured his readers of his conscientious effort to sift truth from falsehood, and to relate as fact only what he knew (or at least believed) on good authority to be true. In cases of doubt he promised the reader that he would preface his remarks with a warning phrase, such as "it was said, it was believed, it was supposed." [25] In that part of the *Memoirs of George II* following 1758 he warned the reader that he had withdrawn somewhat from politics at that time, and was no longer so close to the events described as in previous years.[26] In the same vein of frankness he told his readers that they could no longer expect first-hand reports of the Parliamentary debates after 1768, when he retired from the House of Commons.[27] He was equally frank about the months in 1765 when he was in France, but he insisted that he received information on current affairs in these months from his cousin General Conway and from others of as good authority.[28] As will appear, Walpole's actual practice in handling evidence fell somewhat short of his professed ideals.

Frequently Walpole indicated where he had first-hand knowledge; where his information came from hearsay he often (but by no means always) named his sources. He saw Lord Waldegrave's memoirs in manuscript, and he read Dodington's diary when it appeared in 1784.[29] But for the most part Walpole's sources were oral. Lord John Russell observed that in the 1770's General Conway and the Duke of Richmond were Walpole's most important sources of political information.[30] Among his other informants were his father, Henry Fox, the Duke of Bedford, Lord Egmont, Lord Frederick Campbell, Lord Bristol, Monsieur Francés, the French ambassador, and Thomas Townshend.[31] Although Walpole carefully indicated his sources in his *Historic Doubts*, the memoirs mostly do not contain such information—one more indication that he considered them to be an informal work. It is possible that in this respect he followed the practice of Voltaire, whom he noted as stating that authorities should be cited except when writing of one's own time.[32]

Emphasis on truthfulness and care in handling evidence were well established historiographic principles, at least as talking points, in Walpole's day. Burnet had declared, "I tell the truth on all occasions, as fully and freely as I upon my best inquiry have been able to find it out; where things appear doubtful, I deliver them with the same uncertainty." [33] Even the biassed Saint-Simon, with whose memoirs Walpole was familiar later in life, had stated, "There can be no good memoirs but such as are absolutely true . . . As regards the trustworthiness of my memoirs, it will be seen that most of the events related in them came under my own observation, and that, when they did not, my information was derived from persons who themselves took

part in them . . . When my information comes from less trustworthy sources I note the fact . . . I have aimed at nothing beyond truth and accuracy." [34] Similar statements appear in Clarendon's history, and in the memoirs of Edmund Ludlow, Richard
Bulstrode, Charlotte Lennox, Lord Hervey, and Wraxall.[35]

Walpole's honesty in laying bare his bias was also in accord
with contemporary practice. In *Last Journals* he admitted that
"in some things I may have been misinformed, and in others,
from my own passions, I may have exaggerated faults." [36] In
the *Memoirs of George II*, in commenting on some of his unfavorable character judgments, he stated that he had received
"trifling offense" from the Duke of Cumberland, Henry Pelham,
and Hardwicke, and that he had been hurt by the actions of
Henry Fox, his uncle "Old" Horace, and the Duke of Devonshire. But he insisted that George II and the Duke of Newcastle
(also harshly portrayed) never gave him "the most distant
cause of dissatisfaction." [37] Such statements had ample precedents. Burnet had warned his readers of his prejudice against
"hot" clergymen, and Bacon had laid it down as a maxim that
a historian should hold his bias in check.[38]

Somewhat defensively, Walpole went on to declare that he
was impartial in his judgments, and that he avoided flattery,
"that frequent poison of histories." [39] He stated, "I would as
soon wish to be rejected for flattering one party, as for blaming
another." [40] Because they wrote panegyrics he found fault with
Pliny, Bacon, Commines, and even Voltaire.[41] He condemned
for their partiality "our annalists" Wilson, Weldon, and Os-
borne.[42] Clarendon, he decided, had been too prone to eulogize:
"His capital fault is, his whole work being a labored justification
of King Charles." [43] On the other hand he praised Robertson
for his impartiality.[44] To Walpole a flattering history was "unpardonable." [45] Its real character was that of a romance, and its
author an imposter.[46] He determined to be unbiassed. "If I
write, I must write facts. The times I describe have neither
been glorious nor fortunate." [47] From this state of mind arose
his insistence that he was impartial in delineating character.
Repeatedly he asserted his fairness in mentioning the faults of
his friends as well as the virtues of his enemies. He stated further

that his character judgments could be substantiated by the very actions of the men judged.[48] On one occasion he exclaimed, "Posterity, this is an impartial picture!" [49] Such an outburst is typical. In his earliest memoirs Walpole had asserted, "I shall appeal to facts, and if posterity finds that I draw characters, inconsistent with known actions or to concurrent testimonies, let me be suspected of prejudice, and doomed to meet incredulity." [50]

Once Walpole admitted, "I have spoken of every party and faction favorably or unfavorably as I thought they deserved . . . and that is all I mean by calling myself impartial." [51] This is a revealing statement, for it suggests that Walpole was more concerned with giving his sincere opinion than with trying to be objective in his judgments. When he spoke of being impartial, he probably meant merely that he would avoid flattery and abstain from being partial to any individual or group.

In insisting on impartiality Walpole was completely in accord with the views of his contemporaries. The chief criticism of his period was directed against satire or panegyric in both history and biography. [52] Hume stated that "the first quality of an historian is to be impartial." [53] Writers on history such as Whalley, Haley, and Hill, as well as such memoir writers as Count Grammont, Cardinal de Retz, and Wraxall all insisted on the absolute necessity for impartiality.[54] Only a few writers, such as Gibbon and Saint-Simon went so far as to maintain that it was impossible to achieve.[55]

It is apparent that the principles of historiography prevalent in the eighteenth century deeply influenced the character of Walpole's memoirs, however much he declared that he was not writing a formal work. He selected his materials according to the prevalent doctrine that politics were the main subject of history. He placed his emphasis on personalities and gossip because he accepted the current belief that men, often acting behind the scenes, were the effective cause of historical events. He tried to distinguish between fact and hearsay, and he proclaimed himself to be impartial, because his contemporaries were all but unanimous in voicing their reverence for truth and in condemning flattery. In each of these respects—selection of subject matter, theory of history, and method—Walpole was abreast of his times, but no more than that. His statements on the subject have a deceptive aura of brilliance mainly because they are well expressed.

Walpole believed that he was qualified by circumstance and by temperament to carry his plan successfully into execution. As a member of Parliament for over 25 years, he was a direct spectator of and occasionally a participant in many of the events described. As the son of a prime minister,[56] he was in a position to obtain either at first hand or on what he considered to be sound authority much "secret history" denied to "the common of mankind." [57] Here he shared Burnet's belief—and one widely held in the eighteenth century—"Of all men those who have themselves been engaged in affairs, are the fittest to write history." [58] That Walpole believed himself to be impartial has been pointed out. As for his literary capabilities, modesty forbade any overt statement. Walpole occasionally denied that he had real genius, such as he attributed to the poet Thomas Gray,[59] but he could hardly have been unaware of his skill as a writer of prose.

The seriousness with which Walpole took his self-imposed task may best be estimated from the huge effort which he expended on his memoirs. Although he spoke of them as "casual" or "cursory" writings, and expressed diffidence at the manner in which they had been "thrown together," [60] the fact remains that for about 45 years they were among the major projects of his life. The texts of the memoirs and journals (which number nine large volumes in print, in addition to the unpublished "Memoires, from the Declaration of the War with Spain" and the "Journal 1783–91") are written in a fair hand, mainly Walpole's, but partly in the hand of his secretary Kirgate—an indication that they were neither casually written nor thrown together. Walpole also profusely annotated his memoirs, much in the same way that he annotated his transcribed copies of his letters to Horace Mann. Despite his self-deprecatory remarks, which may be discounted as affected modesty, Walpole took enormous pains with his work. The extent of his labors may be taken as evidence of his entire sincerity of purpose.

Walpole's memoirs, then, are the result of a carefully conceived plan, executed according to contemporary critical standards by a man who believed himself capable of presenting a trustworthy account of the main political events of his own time. How far he succeeded he left to the judgment of posterity.

3.

....

Walpole's Style of Historical Writing

POSTERITY HAS MADE sharply conflicting evaluations of Walpole's trustworthiness as a reporter of political events. On the one hand a number of historians and critics have rejected his work as unreliable. Macaulay stated in the *Edinburgh Review* for October, 1833, "Everybody who reads his works with attention will find that they swarm with loose and foolish observations . . . which might pass in conversation or in a hasty letter, but which are unpardonable in books deliberately written and repeatedly corrected." [1] Hallam concluded that Walpole's "want of accuracy, or veracity, or both, is so palpable that no great stress can be laid on his testimony." [2] Stanhope's verdict was equally severe: "The authority of Horace Walpole will seldom weigh much with a dispassionate historian, unless when confirmed, or at least, not opposed by others." [3] Bancroft believed that Walpole's testimony was "not decisive." [4] Lecky spoke of him in disparaging terms, as did Hawke's biographer, Montagu Burrows.[5] Croker, the editor and critic, wrote a series of articles on Walpole which are no less savage than Macaulay's.[6] Lord Holland, editor of Walpole's *Memoirs of George II*, has stated that the quality of Walpole's character analyses "shakes one's confidence either in his judgment or in his integrity." [7] It is interesting to note as well that George III, who read the letters in volume five of Walpole's *Works*, commented that some of them were not strictly accurate in detail.[8]

On the other hand several recent historians have commented on Walpole's accuracy in his reports of specific political episodes.

Namier has noted that Walpole received reliable political information from General Conway in the 1760's and that his analysis of the nomenclature of political parties in 1768 was correct.[9] Butterfield and Pares have commended Walpole's treatment of several political episodes in the 1760's.[10] Butterfield has also stated that Walpole's information on the Yorkshire reform movement of 1779–80 was usually accurate although not complete.[11]

Despite these conflicting judgments, the fact remains that virtually every writer on eighteenth-century English history has used Walpole's memoirs and letters, though with varying degrees of reserve. It has been remarked that "over a hundred years ago historical writers began to use him as the chief authority on his period. Since then a great many of them appear to have used no other." [12] In the first place, Walpole's accounts are colorful and eminently quotable. Secondly, his work covers so great a period of time and touches on such a variety of subjects that the temptation is almost irresistible to take one's material from it rather than to consult other scattered sources. His memoirs have been, and doubtless will continue to be, regarded as one of the standard sources of the history of eighteenth-century England. For this reason a revaluation of his reliability is particularly desirable.

A major difficulty in determining the accuracy of Walpole's reports arises from his style of writing. The central fact about Walpole is that he was a creative artist of high order. Much that otherwise might be obscure and mysterious in his character becomes intelligible when one acknowledges his unmistakable literary genius. Both the merits and defects of his memoirs largely arise from this aspect of his personality.

As a young man he had ambitions of being a poet, and although eventually he decided that he did not have outstanding poetic talent, during his lifetime he wrote much fugitive verse which is not without charm.[13] It may be recalled that he wrote a tragedy, a comedy, and a novel, but his real genius appears in the prose artistry of his correspondence and memoirs, artistry not surpassed in the eighteenth century.

Walpole's letters are incomparable. The eighteenth-century gentleman regarded gracious conversation and brilliant correspondence as a part of good manners. Walpole was especially successful as a letter writer not only because he was born an aristocrat and a prose artist but also because he cultivated his talent. The practise of writing thousands of letters brought to his style a polish lacking in his earlier attempts. His letters are outstanding because of his variety of interests and because each correspondence was a sustained effort, having a continuity lacking in the so-called occasional letter. Also Walpole's correspondents were largely removed from the scenes described in the letters, so that in relating events he was not repeating matters mutually familiar. Mann lived in Florence, Madame du Deffand in Paris, Gray in Cambridge, Mason in Yorkshire, and Montagu in a series of country estates—all removed from the panorama of life in London and its environs which Walpole so brilliantly portrayed.

Walpole's artistic purpose is implicit in his work, in that the reader should be entertained not only by the subject matter but also by the way in which the story was told. His preoccupation with presenting a vivid narrative is apparent in the following passages from his memoirs:

"I might have made it [the memoirs] more uniform by correction, but the natural *coloring* would have been lost; . . . as it stands an *original sketch*, it is at least a *picture* of my own mind and opinions. Nothing can *paint* the importance of this victory to the court so strongly as what the Princess of Wales said. Whatever *pictures* shall be *drawn* of him [Hardwicke] where those *lines* do not predominate, will be unlike, false, and flattering. But they [anecdotes] contain that most useful part of all history, a *picture* of human minds. Yet it was the duty of an annalist, and of a *painter* of nature, to exhibit the varying features of his [Chatham's] *portrait*. The *lights* and *shades* of a great character are a moral lesson. But it must be remembered that I am *painting a portrait* of the times, rather than writing history." [14]

Such metaphors taken from the graphic arts give a clue to Walpole's artistic purpose. Walpole's contemporaries also saw in history more than a mere record. Voltaire thought of it as a drama, while Bolingbroke and Chesterfield conceived it to be

mainly a storehouse of moral examples.[15] Walpole tended to
share these views, and in a passage earlier than any of those
quoted above he made a revealing admission: "The picture of
so memorable an era drawn by an eye witness must, with all
its faults and prejudices, be more striking to future readers,
than the cold and critical detail which men less partial may
hereafter retrace and digest on a regular plan." [16] It seems clear
here that Walpole preferred to be "striking" and partial rather
than cold and unprejudiced. In another place Walpole elaborated this concept. "They who write of their own times love
or hate the actors, and draw you to their party; but with the
fear of the *laws* of history before his eyes, a compiler affects
you no more than a chancery suit about the entail of an estate
with whose owners you was not acquainted. Poor Lord Lyttelton
was of that tribe the most circumspect, and consequently the
most insipid. His *Henry II* raises no more passions than Burn's
Justice of the Peace." [17] Here the inference may be drawn that
a circumspect account, compiled according to strict historical
"laws," is insipid, therefore less desirable than a biassed narrative that excites the passions.

One recalls Walpole's characterization of the Medieval
chroniclers as "dry"; his statement that formal histories were
"weighty"; his comment to Mary Berry on history, that "without
some romance it is but a register of crimes and calamities";
and his remark to Pinkerton, "I hate the cold impartiality recommended to historians." [18] Despite Walpole's protestations that
he revered truth, he preferred a biassed and highly colored
narrative to one which was accurate and unexciting.

Walpole's preference was one of taste, and is consistent
with his own aesthetic leanings. Essentially it is a literary judgment, as if he were criticizing a novel, a poem, or a play. He
often commented on the literary styles of memorialists and
historians. Torcy's memoirs he found "dry," and those of Bach-
aumont "ill written." [19] He praised Gibbon's style; terming it
"smooth as a Flemish picture." [20] He admired Hume's prose as
well as that of Clarendon.[21] In some degree here Walpole was
in harmony with contemporary opinion, for in the eighteenth
century it was usual to speak of history as a branch of literature.[22]

But Walpole's contemporaries mainly put accuracy first, while his criterion throughout tended to be one of artistry instead of exactitude. This aspect of Walpole's opinion has profound implications with respect to his own work.

Those passages in which the reader is made to feel the drama of an event Walpole almost certainly regarded as his most successful writing. He all but said so himself: "The spirit of the times, and the characters of the men who gave color to events, being almost my sole objects in these memoirs." [23] That he succeeded in presenting a colorful narrative few can deny. Walpole's real forte was descriptive writing, building an incident by careful selection of detail, until it burst into life.

Even Croker, whose feelings toward Walpole were far from sympathetic, admitted that he had revolutionized the reporting of Parliamentary debates, which are, so Croker stated, "painted with a spirit and a force, of which the ordinary style of reporting could not convey the slightest idea." [24] The following passages from Walpole's memoirs illustrate Croker's meaning:

"This philippic was uttered with every vehemence of language and gesture: the bitterest terms flowing spontaneously from him [James Grenville] who had ever been the most obscure and unready speaker: and what added to the outrage of the diction was, that sitting on the bench immediately above Rigby, and dashing about his arm in the air, he seemed to aim blows at the latter, who was forced to crouch lest he should receive them." [25]

"The very uncertainty whether Mr. Pitt's health would allow him to attend, concurred to augment the impatience of the public on so serious a crisis . . . Beckford proposed to refer the preliminaries [of the Peace of 1763] to a Committee of the Whole House . . . The demand was opposed by Ellis, Sir Francis Dashwood, and Harris of Salisbury, when the House was alarmed by a shout from without! The doors opened, and at the head of a large acclaiming concourse was seen Mr. Pitt, borne in the arms of his servants, who, setting him down within the bar, he crawled by the help of a crutch, and with the assistance of some few friends, to his seat. . . . He was dressed in black velvet, his legs and thighs wrapped in flannel, his feet covered with buskins of black cloth, and his hands with thick gloves." [26]

As an accurate writer Walpole was less successful. Brilliant writing and precise writing require abilities of entirely different sorts. The former calls for a highly developed imagination; the latter demands a highly disciplined mind. As a literary artist, Walpole had extraordinary imaginative faculties, but his capabilities as a thinker were not so highly developed. The very talents which made him a brilliant writer in large measure prevented him from being an accurate reporter.

He lacked discipline, and this want was as much the result of his environment as of his temperament. As a member of the English aristocracy, he was completely secure socially. By virtue of the sinecure places obtained for him by his father, he had a secure income.[27] As a child, he was pampered.[28] As a confirmed bachelor, he escaped the conflicts and responsibilities of marriage and parenthood. Being secure both socially and economically, he shared in that freedom of self-expression which is among the most prominent characteristics of an aristocratic way of life.[29] As a bachelor aristocrat, he was among the freest of the free.

Walpole himself admitted that he was impractical. "I never had a head or an inclination for business," he wrote, "and have passed an idle life in amusing myself with trifles—nor do I regret my option." [30] As a youth he was incapable of learning mathematics.[31] He stated that he had little understanding of theology, philosophy, astronomy, and political economy.[32] As he observed, "I understand nothing useful. My head is as un-mechanic as it is un-arithmetic, un-geometric, un-metaphysic, un-commercial." [33] Although entered at Lincoln's Inn, Walpole soon revealed that he had no inclination for the law, which he was fond of ridiculing in later life.[34] Understandably he developed his native talents and neglected those fields of knowledge unconnected with his own special gifts.

Walpole justified his action by a rationalization common among artists. "Scorn rules, Sir, that cramp genius," he once remarked.[35] Creative artists often revolt against conventional restraints and insist on complete freedom of self-expression. In Walpole's time this revolt was directed against classicism, and the drive toward untrammeled self-expression took form in "Gothicism," an earlier phase of the romantic movement. Walpole's intellectual limitations and his rationalization of them in artistic terms are apparent in his work. He preferred sensibility to sense. Matters of taste were more important to him than matters of intellect, which he considered to be pedantic and cold. His philosophic passages are somewhat awkward, but he was indifferent to this deficiency in his writing. "Philosophy," he once declared, "is only a matter of muscles. I never could command mine." [36] For Newton, "a great star-gazer and conjurer," as well as for Euclid and Locke, he had "sovereign contempt," adding that he admired only "original genius." [37] In a characteristic passage he explained his view fully: "*No man was ever yet so great as to build that system in which other men could not discover flaws. All our reasoning, therefore, is very imperfect, and this is my reason for being so seldom serious, and for never disputing. I look upon human reason as I do on the parts of a promising child—it surprises, may improve or stop short, but is not come to maturity; and therefore, if you please, I will talk of the Birthday, and things more suited to my capacity.*" [38] His decision was clear. "I had rather have written the two speeches of Lady Percy, in the second part of *Henry IV,* than all Voltaire." [39] These judgments reflect his own capabilities, for he was at his best in dashing off a literary *jeu d'esprit,* at his worst in spinning out a closely reasoned argument.[40] Analysis and criticism, except as they were part of the process of artistic selectivity, had little place in his usual literary expression.

Macaulay's stricture on Walpole's "loose and foolish observations" is not without justice. At times his use of antithesis, exaggeration, and innuendo seriously distorts his narrative.

Walpole's use of antithesis is unfortunate. In contrasting the influence of the *Craftsman* and the satires of Sir Charles Hanbury Williams, he stated, "Sir Charles remained a steady friend to [Sir Robert] Walpole, and persecuted his rival, Lord Bath, in a succession of satiric odes, that did more execution in six months, than the Craftsman had done in twice the number of years; for the minister only lost his power, but the patriot

his character." [41] A student of English political journalism will
have difficulty with this passage. It cannot be taken literally
to mean what it says. Elsewhere Walpole wrote another version.
"The pen of Sir Charles Hanbury Williams inflicted deeper
wounds in three months on this Lord [Bath], than a series of
Craftsmen, aided by Lord Bolingbroke for several years, could
imprint on Sir Robert Walpole. The latter lost his power, but
lived to see justice done to his character. His rival acquired
no power, but—died very rich." [42] Here Walpole said something
quite different: that three months of Williams' satires were more
effective than the *Craftsman* for "several years." He also omitted
mention of the destruction of Lord Bath's character. It is obvious
that this is the less "literary" of the two versions.

That the second passage was written for publication in his
Royal and Noble Authors, where it would be subject to the
criticism of his contemporaries, may or may not be significant.
But it is important to notice that the version which appears in
his memoirs differs from the other version, not in greater intellectual depth, but in greater literary polish. In other words,
Walpole placed his emphasis rather on verbal artistry than on
trying to convey a more exact meaning.

Walpole's antithetical passage on Pelham and Sir Robert
Walpole is equally unfortunate. "Sir Robert Walpole was bold,
open, steady, never dejected . . . Mr. Pelham was timorous,
reserved, fickle, apt to despair. . . . Sir Robert Walpole loved
power so much, that he would not endure a rival; Mr. Pelham
loved it so well, that he would endure anything. . . . The one
was honored by his enemies, the other at best pitied by his
friends. . . . The one durst do right and durst do wrong too;
the other dared either so little, that it generally ended in his
doing the latter. . . . Both were loved in private life. . . . All men
thought Mr. Pelham honest till he was in power; the other was
never thought so till he was out." [43] This long passage, in part
quoted above, is an interesting example of eighteenth-century
antithetical writing. But to take meaning from it is not easy.

Walpole fell into the same sort of misleading prose in contrasting Henry Fox and the elder Pitt. "Fox always spoke to
the question, Pitt to the passions: Fox, to carry the question;

Pitt, to raise himself: Fox pointed out, Pitt lashed the errors of his antagonists: Pitt's talents were likely to make him soonest, Fox's to keep him First Minister longest." [44] The student of history has only to find one passionate speech of Fox to deprive this passage of much of its meaning. A final instance may be cited. "Instead of sending men, arms, ammunition to the invaded frontiers of our colonies, with more partriarchal vigilance his Royal Highness [the Prince of Wales] sent them an hundred pounds of Leland's polemic writings against the deists." [45] Both Lord Holland and Macaulay have pointed out that the Prince of Wales had neither the means nor the duty of sending men, arms, and ammunition to the colonies.[46]

Such antithetical passages cannot be taken literally, and are instances where Walpole's desire to be literary has vitiated the intelligibility of what he wrote. They appear most frequently in the earlier memoirs. By 1759 Walpole was aware of the undesirability of excessive antithesis,[47] and for the most part he abandoned this misleading device in his later writings.

A second distortion appears in Walpole's use of exaggeration. The following instances illustrate this tendency in his work: "Lord Chief Justice Willes was . . . always browbeaten by haughty Yorke. Dr. Middleton, the best writer of the age, had overturned the Fathers. Lawyers . . . make a trade of perplexing. The City of London, always governed by the absurdest heads in it. . . . Lawyers never suffer correction of abuses; they defend them even where they do not commit them. Pride, revenge, and avarice were his [Hardwicke's] true features; and whatever pictures shall be drawn of him where those lines do not predominate, will be unlike, false, and flattering. The Marquis of Tavistock . . . died at the age of twenty-seven. . . . All mankind who ever heard the name of Lord Tavistock were profuse in lamenting such a national calamity. No great country was ever saved by honest men from arbitrary power." [48] These and other similar exaggerations require little comment. Needless to say, they represent a mood of temporary enthusiasm rather than seasoned reflection.

Many of Walpole's analyses require a critical approach. Discussing the general election of 1761 he stated: "It had been

propagated that the king had forbidden any money to be issued
from the Treasury. Nothing was less true, in fact, or proved
less true in effect. Both the Court and particulars went greater
length than in any preceding times. In truth, the corruption of
electors met, if not exceeded that of candidates. The borough of
Sudbury was so shameless as to advertise itself to the highest
bidder." [49] This paragraph contains an error in fact which caused
Walpole to make two incorrect statements, for it is now known
from examination of secret-service accounts that no money was
expended by the Treasury (under George III) on the general
election of 1761.[50] It follows that the court did not go "greater
length" in corruption than in any preceding times.

Aside from Walpole's error in fact, his remarks are misleading and illustrative of his use of innuendo.[51] A hasty reading
of the above passage leaves the impression that the Crown had
professed virtue while in fact indulging in unprecedented
venality. Actually (even disregarding his basic error) Walpole
has not made his point, for in an emotional rather than a
logical sequence of ideas he proceeded from Crown corruption
to the corruption of candidates and electors—which has no
bearing on the Crown's activities. But by stating that the election
itself was corrupt, he has left the impression that the Crown
also was corrupt, although the proof offered has no relation
to the original proposition. What, for instance, has Sudbury's
advertising itself for sale to do with George III?

A similar instance of distortion appears in the "Journal
1783–91" for the month of December, 1783: "Lord Spencer who
loved Pitt, tried too, to reconcile him and Fox, but Pitt behaved
so haughtily, that he lost Lord Spencer's friendship, who thence
attached himself more strongly to Fox." The reader receives
two impressions, one, that Lord Spencer initiated the negotiation; and two, that it was broken off because of Pitt's haughtiness.
Quite the contrary happened. It was Pitt who first communicated with Lord Spencer, and it was Fox who broke off the
negotiation after consulting with his friends. There is no hint
in Lord Spencer's correspondence that Pitt's behavior had
offended him, but a letter of Sir Gilbert Elliot reveals how

offensive Pitt's proposal was to Fox and to the Whig group as a whole, which of course included Horace Walpole.[52]

A further instance of inexact writing appears in the *Memoirs of George III*, where Walpole stated, "So true was the maxim of Sir Robert Walpole, that every man has his price." [53] Elsewhere Walpole was more circumspect. On two occasions he mentioned this saying as merely attributed to his father, without avowing or denying it, and on a third he ascribed it to his father's enemies.[54] Finally, on at least two occasions Walpole denied that he had ever heard his father make such a statement, and he went so far as to express the belief that "no such expression ever came from his mouth." [55] Walpole's various remarks on this maxim are not consistent, and the blunt ascription of it in the memoirs to his father, without qualification or comment, is misleading.

It appears from the foregoing instances that Walpole was liable to color his writing at the expense of exactitude, that sometimes his prose was marred by antithesis and exaggeration, and that at other times his analyses and narratives were emotionally rather than logically constructed, with the result that the reader receives a false impression. Such writing might be admirable in a purely literary production, where the intention of the writer is to evoke interest. It is less suited to memoirs intended as accurate narratives of political events.

4.

....

Walpole's Character Sketches

By his own testimony Walpole was a man of deep feelings and almost ungovernable temper. It is difficult to understand the judgment of Lecky and Feiling that he had a "cold heart." [1] One of his favorite sayings reveals his sensitivity, "This world is a comedy to those who think, a tragedy to those who feel." [2] According to his self-portrait he had "a warm conception, vehement attachments, strong aversions." [3] He avowed his "strong prejudices" to Lady Ossory, and upon another occasion told her that the "Walpole temper" was violent.[4] Early in life he spoke of his "natural ferocity and wildness," and to Lord Harcourt he confessed, "I know how strong my prejudices are, and am always afraid of them." [5]

Walpole's contemporaries were well aware of the warmth of his feelings. In 1756 his "ardor" for intrigue annoyed Richard Rigby.[6] He impressed Cole and Gray with his violence as a party politician, and once, during the American War, George Selwyn remarked that he was "as peevish as a monkey." [7]

One of the most dramatic passages in the memoirs described the "agony" he suffered during his vain attempt to save the life of Admiral Byng.[8] When, in April, 1764, his cousin and idol General Conway lost his regiment for voting against general warrants, Walpole was "stunned" and retired into the country for three days to compose his rage.[9] In the summer following, while in a state of emotional tension, in part brought on by his distress at Conway's dismissal, he wrote his *Castle of Otranto*, a novel which can hardly be described as a calm production.[10]

42

Leslie Stephen has observed that he was "a touchy companion."[11] Although it is possible to overemphasize this aspect of his personality, he quarreled with many of his friends, such as Gray, Ashton, Thomas Pitt, Henry Fox, Lord Harcourt, and Mason. In 1770 he and George Montagu parted precipitately, the exact cause of their rupture being unknown. With his uncle "Old" Horace he had a dispute over the marriage of Margaret Nichol, an unsavory episode in which there was much heated conduct on both sides.[12] The justice of Walpole's attitude in each of these episodes need not be here examined; it is enough to point out that the episodes were numerous.

Further evidence of the depth of Walpole's emotions appears in the many letters of despair which he wrote during the years of the American Revolution, which contrast sharply with the carefree tone of his previous correspondence, and in his equally vociferous outbursts against the French Revolution.[13] Occasionally he vented his feelings in rhetorical expressions, such as the following: "Our descendants will see what their ancestors were in arms and eloquence, and what liberty they enjoyed of discussing their own interests. Grant, Heaven, that they may not read it with a sigh; reading it in bondage and ignominy. What a trade is the politician's, when it can so debase the human mind! Comfort yourself, ye poor, ye necessitous; what is the servility of your lot compared to this of titles and riches? O man! man! dare not to vaunt your virtue, while self-interest lurks in every pore."[14]

Walpole's strong feelings permeate his memoirs. In fact, the emotionalism present, especially in his character judgments, has often been cited as one of their least pleasant features. Lord Ossory, who read them in manuscript, was appalled: "Mr. Walpole's memoirs are lively and entertaining, but, considering that he was apparently a very good natured man, it is surprizing to find them so full of bitterness and malignity. . . . I should regret these being published, or even much seen, as I cannot think they do him much honor or credit, and are most scurrilous upon many characters."[15] Lord Ossory's view, the earliest recorded criticism of the memoirs, has been echoed by Walpole's editors, Lord Holland and Lord Dover, and by his most recent biographer, Ketton-Cremer, to say nothing of numerous other commentators whose knowledge of Walpole's work was less profound.[16]

A few examples of Walpole's character judgments may be given:

Lord Barrington: "The dirty little creature." [17]

Charles Churchill: "This bacchanalian priest, now mouthing patriotism, and now venting libertinism, the scourge of bad men, and scarce better than the worst, debauching wives, and protecting his gown by the weight of his fist." [18]

Lord Gower: "A villain capable of any crime." [19]

Samuel Johnson: "With a lumber of learning and some strong parts, Johnson was an odious and mean character. By principle a Jacobite, arrogant, self-sufficient, and overbearing by nature, ungrateful through pride and of *feminine bigotry,* he had prostituted his pen to party . . . His manners were sordid, supercilious, and brutal, his style ridiculously bombastic and vicious; and, in one word, with all the pedantry he had all the gigantic littleness of a country schoolmaster." [20]

Robert Nugent "had set out ill in virtue by marrying an old rich widow to the impoverishment of her son." [21]

Sir William Pynsent had "not many scruples; living to her death with his only daughter in pretty notorious incest." [22]

Lord Shelburne was "ready for any crimes that suited his plans." [23]

"Old" Horace Walpole: "His mind was a strange mixture of sense alloyed by absurdity, wit by mimicry, knowledge by buffoonery, bravery by meanness, honesty by selfishness . . . His body was more uniform, for that was throughout burlesque and uncouth." [24]

Philip Carteret Webb: "A most villainous tool and agent in any iniquity." [25]

Nineteenth-century critics reacted unfavorably to this sort of invective, and twentieth-century readers are equally unsympathetic. It would be easy to dismiss Walpole's judgments as the ebullitions of a spiteful mind, but this would be to oversimplify and to make the false assumption that the same standards obtained in his time as in a later period. Although the character judgments appear to be so over-colored that they become almost meaningless, as Lord Dover observed,[26] they nevertheless represent a type of polemic which was commonplace in the eighteenth century. George II, for example, did not hesitate to vilify his political opponents in extravagant terms, and Queen Caroline, in speaking of her son, the Prince of Wales, was even less gentle in her invective.[27] Such violence was by no means extraordinary. To find its counterpart one has only to read Pope's satires and the columns of abuse, such as Junius' letters, in the daily newspapers, or to glance through a collection of contemporary political cartoons, which were invariably brutal and occasionally obscene. It was customary to prove that one's opponent was wrong by proving that he was wicked.[28]

The tone of unrestraint pervaded the Houses of Parliament as a phase of oratorical eloquence. The classical tradition in oratory flourished during the eighteenth century. Cicero, Aristotle, and Quintilian, in that order, enjoyed vast popularity as classical authorities on eloquence, and throughout the century a considerable number of English treatises appeared on the subject.[29] Chesterfield was particularly emphatic that his son should master the art of oratory, asserting that "No man can make a fortune or a figure in this country, without speaking, and speaking well, in public." [30] He attributed the success of Chancellor Cowper and the elder Pitt to their elegant language, which impressed their audience despite the weakness of many of their arguments.[31] Corroboration of Chesterfield's view is not far to seek. The first three speeches of the younger Pitt in the House of Commons convinced many of his hearers that he would soon occupy a "high situation" in the government.[32] With oratory regarded as a main avenue to political success, the classical tradition persisted, and interest in public speaking remained widespread. Although himself an ineffective speaker,[33] Walpole was concerned with the oratorical capabilities of his contemporaries to the extent of writing a survey of the leading debaters in George II's time, and in 1772 he made a special visit to the House of Commons to hear Charles James Fox.[34]

In many respects the oratory was highly artificial. With the emphasis placed on eloquence rather than on coherence of

argument, politicians ranted and delivered themselves of philippics, and occasionally chatted with the object of their invective
when the formal proceedings ended.[35] Burke broke off his friendship with Fox during a debate in the House of Commons, an
occasion for open weeping, and another time adopted the the-
atrical expedient of throwing down a dagger when he reached
the climax of his speech.[36] Chatham was notorious for his
dramatic speeches.[37] Besides, it was not unknown for speakers
to harangue their audience while a little in liquor.[38] In short,
one put on heroic buskins and acted out an epic role in a melo-
dramatic atmosphere.

That Walpole thought of politics in terms of drama appears
in the following passages: "Intrigues of the Cabinet, or of
Parliament, scarce existed at that period. . . . Few new *characters*
appeared upon the *stage*. No man is acquainted with the whole
plot. . . . Yet, partial as the narratives of the *actors* must be,
they will certainly approach nearer to truth than those of
spectators. They who write of their own times love or hate the
actors. In short, I think my winter will be very well amused,
whether Mr. Garrick and Mr. Pitt act or not."[39] Being both
sensitive and volatile, Walpole was affected more than most
men by the impact of such a drama, and he became emotionally
involved to a high degree in the political issues of his day.

Some of Walpole's contemporaries preserved more *sang froid*.
Writing to his son, Sir James Harris stated, "Burke was diffuse
and eloquent. I who am used to order, and study no books but
such as have a beginning, middle, and end, cannot relish a
rhapsody, however exquisite, and . . . I smile at the mock
tragedy, when perhaps at Drury Lane I should weep."[40] A
reaction gradually set in against the hyperbolic and lengthy
speeches, which grew increasingly common in the last quarter
of the eighteenth century.[41] In 1781 the Speaker noticed that
some members absented themselves from the debate and entered
the House only to vote, and in 1788 George III urged "the
friends of government to speak merely to the point in future, and
try to shorten debates, and bring if possible the present bad
mode of mechanical oratory into discredit."[42] But to Walpole
politics remained so exciting that they were "painful." He added,

"and though I have nothing to do with them, the ill humor they occasion, and the perpetual discourse on them, are exceedingly disagreeable to one whose whole wishes are centered in repose." [43] Accordingly Walpole gave up his seat in the House of Commons when he was fifty-one years old, but he was never able to detach himself emotionally from the political scene. All that he did in his memoirs was to record faithfully the political animosities of his period, with all their passion and unreason, and to leave to posterity a series of character judgments written in the conventional political idiom of his own time. To find fault with the quality of Walpole's judgments to to quarrel with the political customs of an entire period of history. It were better to discover the pattern of his likes and dislikes, and to find out what his criteria were.

Several dominant themes emerge. The main theme of the *Memoirs of George II* was a panegyric of his father's administration. Walpole worshipped his father, who he believed (in 1758) was one of the five great men of his time.[44] To Mann in 1779 he stated, "My father is ever before my eyes—not to attempt to imitate him, for I have none of his matchless wisdom, or unsullied virtues, or heroic firmness." [45] Walpole admitted that he was unable to be impartial about Sir Robert, and because of his partiality he consistently refused to undertake his father's biography.[46] In his various writings he noted only a few of Sir Robert's failings: that he was indelicate with women, occasionally coarse in his language, and that his "foible" was inattention to foreign affairs.[47] Walpole's veneration for his father was well known to his contemporaries, one of whom remarked that it was "amiable, but in the outrage of it absurd." [48]

Occasionally Walpole compared his father to the politicians of a later period. Thus, Sir Robert was Pelham's "master" in finance, and Thomas Potter only imitated him in wishing to revive the excise.[49] Once he compared his father favorably to the Duke of Grafton, who "could not bear the thoughts of business . . . I could but reflect how different had been the application of Sir Robert Walpole." [50] But such passages are infrequent, and a better index of Walpole's devotion to his father appears in his characterization of his father's political opponents:

Chesterfield, Lord Bath, Pelham, Lord Granville, Newcastle, Hardwicke, and the elder Pitt.

Walpole's main contention about Chesterfield was that his reputation for wit was unfounded. Walpole insisted that Chesterfield's name would survive chiefly in almanacs because of his reform of the calendar, "when the wit that he had but labored too much . . . will be no more remembered." [51] The key to the tone of Walpole's remarks appears in his statement that Chesterfield had opposed Sir Robert Walpole and had urged his impeachment.[52]

Walpole was more severe on Lord Bath. He stated that the satires of Sir Charles Hanbury Williams had destroyed Lord Bath's reputation.[53] He also spoke of Lord Bath's "ambition, treachery, irresolution, timidity, and want of judgment." [54] His further comment is suggestive: "Who does not know that Mr. Pulteney [Lord Bath] was the great rival of Sir Robert Walpole, whose power he so long opposed, at last overturned, and was undone with it?" [55]

Something of Walpole's opinion of Pelham appears in the long antithetical passage, previously discussed, where Pelham is stated to be timid, fickle, unscrupulous, and generally tending to evil.[56] The reason for Walpole's hostility is not far to seek. In his autobiographic notes Walpole commented, "Mr. Pelham had used my father and his friends extremely ill." [57]

Lord Granville fared little better. Although Walpole termed him one of the five great men of the age and praised both his eloquence and scholarship, he characterized Lord Granville as rash, contemptuous, extravagant, and unlovable.[58] Walpole did not conceal his motives. Granville, so he believed, had early tried to "undermine" Sir Robert Walpole, and had "hurried into power" after Sir Robert's fall.[59]

In the memoirs the Duke of Newcastle appears as an object of comedy. Walpole's ridicule is unremitting: "His person was not naturally despicable; his incapacity, his mean soul, and the general low opinion of him, grew to make it appear ridiculous." Walpole added, "Fear, a ridiculous fear, was predominant in him." [60] In a letter to Mann he commented, "who would not laugh at a world, where so ridiculous a creature as the Duke of

Newcastle can overturn ministries!" [61] Elsewhere he caricatured Newcastle as having "the monkey disposition of Heliogabalus." [62] The root of Walpole's hostility is all too apparent: "Towards the decline of Sir Robert Walpole's ministry, the Duke of Newcastle, who feared to fall with him, and hoped to rise upon his ruins, dealt largely with the Opposition, to compass both." [63]

The character sketch of Lord Hardwicke in the memoirs represents a high point in Walpole's invective. Only the portrait of Lord Mansfield equals it in severity. Walpole wrote, "Sir Philip Yorke, Baron of Hardwicke, and Lord Chancellor, was a man of low birth, and lower principles. He was a creature of the Duke of Newcastle. . . . In the House of Lords he was laughed at; in the Cabinet despised. . . . His exceeding parsimony was qualified by his severity to and discouragement of usurers and gamesters. . . . The best thing that can be remembered of the Chancellor is his fidelity to his patron; for let the Duke of Newcastle betray whom he would, the Chancellor always stuck to him in his perfidy, and was only not false to the falsest of mankind." [64] Philip Yorke has stated that Walpole's aversion to Hardwicke may have originated in the "trifling offense" which Walpole received from him, possibly connected with some re-arrangement of Walpole's sinecures, or because Hardwicke was friendly with "Old" Horace Walpole, with whom Walpole had quarreled.[65] A more probable cause of Walpole's animosity appears in his belief that Hardwicke had contributed to Sir Robert Walpole's fall.[66]

Walpoles' characterization of the elder Pitt was not wholly sympathetic. On the one hand he named Pitt as one of the five great men of his time, praised his oratorical abilities, and gave him full credit for the statesmanship which enhanced the glory of England in the Seven Years War.[67] Otherwise Walpole was singularly unflattering: as an orator Pitt spoke too often and too long; as a war minister he was ignorant of finance and squandered too much money on military operations.[68] Walpole also objected to Pitt's "wanton exposure" of human life in the expeditions against the French coast, adding that Pitt's "thirst of glory was inconsistent with humanity." [69] Above all Walpole deplored Pitt's ambition and haughtiness, which he termed

"Persian grandeur." [70] Much of Walpole's animosity resulted from Pitt's coolness to Walpole's cousin, General Conway, but in large measure it proceeded from Pitt's opposition to Sir Robert Walpole.[71]

A second main theme of Walpole's memoirs was a spirited justification of his own and Conway's political conduct. Walpole was fond of announcing that he had never given a vote because of influence, that except for those of his father he had attended the levee of only one minister (Newcastle), when Sir Robert Walpole was in power, that he had never received a favor for himself from any minister except his father, and that in general his political activity revealed his independence, disinterestedness, and lack of personal ambition.[72] Occasionally he felt called upon to justify his tenure of sinecures, obtained for him by his father, which he did by adopting the "comfortable doctrines" that patent places were sanctioned by law and custom, and that so long as there was an unequal distribution of wealth, "some will be more fortunate than others." [73] Walpole went further and declared that his conduct in administering the sinecures had been as honest as his other political acts.[74]

Walpole announced that on two occasions he had been approached with offers to grant him his share in the office of Collector of the Customs for life, instead of holding it only so long as his brother Edward lived. Henry Fox made the first offer, after Pelham's death when Fox joined Newcastle, and Lord North made the second in 1775. Walpole refused both offers. He also had an oblique offer from Lord Bute, which he declined.[75] In his formal account of his conduct relative to his places, written to justify his actions, Walpole stated that because his brother Edward was eleven years his senior, and because his eldest brother Robert, third Earl of Orford, was "declining," his friends urged him to ask Pelham to have his patent place in the Custom House secured for life. Walpole demurred, but "at last" saw Pelham, who refused the request unless the patent were revised in such a way that Edward Walpole would lose considerably if Horace should pre-decease him. This proposal Horace Walpole rejected, commenting, "This was in the year

1751, and was the first and last favor I ever asked of any minister for myself." [76]

Citing Walpole's letter to Pelham of November 25, 1752, with Walpole's attached notes, Romney Sedgwick has tried to prove that Walpole's statement was incorrect, that in fact Walpole renewed his application to Pelham on December 3, 1752, and met a second refusal, under the same terms as the first interview. Sedgwick commented, "How unbearable he found the recollection of his unsuccessful applications to Pelham can be gathered from the fantasy which he ultimately substituted for them. . . . Horace Walpole succeeded in persuading himself that . . . his rejected solicitations had been improper proposals which he had virtuously refused." [77]

A review of the evidence, on which this adverse judgment is based, suggests that it is possible to go too far in impugning Walpole's testimony. It appears far more likely that Walpole had only one interview with Pelham about his patent place. The similarity of proposal, refusal, counter-proposal, and counter-refusal in both of Walpole's versions of the interview lead to the conclusion that in writing his formal account, thirty years later, he predated the interview by one year and wrote 1751 instead of 1752. Walpole was often careless with dates. This explanation appears the more reasonable in view of his positive assertion that it was the only favor which he had asked *for himself*, a carefully written statement, for he had asked a favor of Grenville for his deputy and for one of his constituents. [78] Besides, this was not a matter about which Walpole was likely to tell a deliberate lie. As for his "fantasy" that he had rejected two "improper proposals," it is apparent that in his letter to Mason of February 2, 1784, which Sedgwick quoted, he was referring not to his interview with Pelham, but to his refusal of offers from Henry Fox and Lord North. Although Walpole's desire to justify his conduct certainly colored his writing, it is believed that he can be acquitted of the charge of intellectual dishonesty and self-deception in relation to his sinecure places.

After the accession of George III in 1760 Walpole mainly dedicated his political activity to furthering his cousin General

Conway's career. Walpole's affection for Conway has been called one of the three deepest emotions of his life.[79] He once declared to Conway, "Since I was fifteen have I not loved you unalterably?"[80] He felt strong gratification in Conway's successes, and suffered pain at Conway's reverses. When Lord John Cavendish threatened Walpole's position as mentor to his cousin, he became jealous. In the memoirs his pique is unconcealed: "Yet before I quitted the scene, I had the pleasure of . . . convincing Lord John Cavendish, that it had been more prudent not to provoke me by attempting to interfere with my influence with Mr. Conway."[81] When Conway was dismissed from his regiment for voting against general warrants, Walpole was hardly able to control his temper. He wrote a pamphlet defending Conway's action, and became embroiled in a heated exchange of letters about Conway with Thomas Pitt which put an end to their friendship.[82] Walpole's apologia for his own and Conway's political conduct, as in the case of his defense of his father, is most graphically revealed in vilification of their political opponents, such as Henry Fox, Bedford, Grenville, and Bute.

At one time Walpole and Henry Fox had been intimate friends, but after 1754, when Fox accepted office under the Duke of Newcastle against Walpole's advice, their relations cooled. It was not long before Walpole began to cast aspersions on Fox's political conduct.[83] He could not fail to have been hurt when Fox refused to help him in his efforts to save Admiral Byng's life, and he disapproved of Fox's behavior when as manager of the House of Commons and a colleague of Lord Bute, Fox (so Walpole believed) used open bribery and gross political persecution to get Parliament to approve the Peace of 1763.[84] Walpole commented, "Fox had boldness and wickedness enough to undertake whatever the Court wished to compass."[85] Elsewhere he spoke of Fox as "cruel, revengeful, daring, and subtle."[86] Although Walpole had ample personal cause for attacking Fox, he noted that for a reason which he did not understand, Fox was a "personal enemy" of General Conway.[87]

Walpole's earlier remarks on the Duke of Bedford, while he and Bedford were on friendly terms, were somewhat sympathetic: that although Bedford was impetuous, obstinate, and conceited, and spoke on too many subjects, Walpole admitted that he spoke readily and was an honest man.[88] Walpole later had occasion to underscore the faults of "the little Duke," emphasizing Bedford's "warmth and absurdities," indiscretion, tyranny, and lack of sensibility on the death of his son.[89] There were several reasons for such a change in emphasis. Walpole noted that Bedford was devoted to Lord Bute, of whose policy he disapproved, and had a share in concluding the Peace of 1763, which he deprecated.[90] On another occasion Walpole stated, "The Bedford faction I knew were my mortal enemies," that is, political opponents. But the chief cause of Walpole's animosity arose from his belief that when Conway's dismissal was proposed, Bedford suggested that Conway be deprived not only of his post in the Bedchamber but of his regiment as well.[91]

There was little restraint in Walpole's characterization of George Grenville, whom he had once described as no less a "Whig Saint" than Algernon Sydney.[92] Under the lash of Walpole's invective Grenville became "the falsest and most contemptible of mankind," "a pedant in politics," "the prater," "that mulish cart-horse," a man of "plodding methodic genius," who spoke too long and practised "tedious tyranny." [93] Although "the ablest man of business" in the House of Commons, Grenville was "bold, proud, dictatorial, and so self-willed that he would have expected Liberty herself should be his first slave." [94] Finally, "scarce any man ever wore in his face such outward and visible marks of the hollow, cruel, and rotten heart within." [95] An important factor in Walpole's animosity was his belief that Grenville had impugned Conway's integrity when Conway voted against general warrants.[96]

Walpole's character sketch of Lord Bute was less severe but on the whole unfavorable. "The Earl of Bute, a Scotchman, who, having no estate, had passed his youth in studying mathematics and mechanics in his own little island, then simples in the hedges about Twickenham, and at five and thirty had fallen in love with his own figure." [97] Walpole added that Bute was "naturally ostentatious of his person, and of haughty carriage," and that he "had a little reading, and affected learning." [98] Elsewhere Walpole mentioned his "incapacity and cowardice," and spoke of his administration as "monarchic and dastardly." [99] As will appear, Walpole detested Bute for ideological reasons, but Bute had also opposed him politically, and Walpole suspected him of complicity in Conway's dismissal.[100]

A third main theme appears in *Last Journals* and in the "Journal 1783–91," which contain a sustained diatribe on the "Tory" ministries of Lord North and the younger Pitt. In *Last Journals* Walpole wrote, "Lord North was a pliant tool, without system or principle; Lord George Germaine of desperate ambition and character; Wedderburn a thorough knave; Lord Sandwich a more profligate knave; Lord Gower a villain capable of any crime; Elliot, Jenkinson, Cornwall, mutes that would have fixed the bowstring round the throat of the constitution." [101] In the "Journal 1783–91" he characterized Pitt's government as "wretched." The Duke of Richmond, Master of the Ordinance, was "capricious and unsteady." The Foreign Secretary, Lord Carmarthen, "had pleasing manners, but no depth, nor character, nor steadiness." The Duke of Dorset, ambassador to France, was unqualified for his post, and Lord Chesterfield, ambassador to Spain, was "a worthless young man, universally despised." Lord Howe was "silly," and Dundas "more decried than all." Walpole continued, "All the rest were children and fools, and Rutland, Chandos, Salisbury, Dorset eminently one or the other." He then praised the abilities and virtues of the members of the Opposition, and concluded that they far outweighed Pitt's "unknown boys." In a word, he found the situation "calamitous." [102]

These three main themes, a panegyric of his father's administration, justification of his own and Conway's political conduct, and a diatribe against the governments of Lord North and the younger Pitt, constitute the most important criteria for the character judgments in Walpole's memoirs and journals. Not all of Walpole's judgments came from these three themes. Some had personal, non-political grounds, such as his dislike for his uncle "Old" Horace, which originated in a family quarrel, and his coolness to Burke, which proceeded as much from snobbery as from his suspicion of Burke's Catholic connections.[103] But the main unifying force in Walpole's judgments of character can be related to his veneration for his father, his belief in his own and Conway's integrity, and his antipathy (a kind of self-justification in reverse) to the "Tory" ministries of North and Pitt.

It is apparent that in writing memoirs Walpole had a hidden third purpose: in addition to his stated intentions of informing and entertaining, he wished to convert the reader to his own political views. If interrogated about the matter, he would probably have replied that he was informing posterity correctly and giving a true portrait of his times, at least as he saw them. But Walpole's projection of his emotions into his work has created a serious distortion and obstacle for scholars interested in using his memoirs and journals as historical sources.

5.

....

The Factual Accuracy of the Memoirs

WALPOLE'S REPORTS OF SPEECHES in Parliament, mainly based on his own notes, are the most authentic part of his memoirs.[1] He himself so considered them, remarking, "I took notes at the time, and have delivered the arguments just as I heard them; never conceiving how it can be proper in a real history to compose orations."[2] The following passages, consisting of Walpole's versions and those of other observers, illustrate the reliability of his reporting:

Debate of January 17, 1751, Walpole's version: "Mr. William Pitt recanted his having seconded the famous question for the *no search* in the last Parliament; said it was a mad and foolish motion, and that he was since grown ten years older and wiser."[3] *Another account:* "Mr. Pitt answered, that he had once been an advocate for that claim [of no search]; it was when he was a young man; but now he was ten years older; had considered public affairs more coolly."[4]

Debate of March 4, 1763, Walpole's version: "That he [Pitt] had a very different opinion from many of the peace; thought it hollow and insecure, and that it would not last ten years."[5] *Another account:* "He called the peace hollow, and not likely to be permanent; he afterwards called it an armed truce for ten years."[6]

Debate of January 14, 1766, Walpole's version: "Will you, after the Peace you have made, and the small pittance of the fishery that is left you, will you sheathe your sword in the bowels of your brothers, the Americans? You may coerce and conquer, but when they fall, they will fall like the strong man embracing the pillars of the Constitution, and bury it in ruin with them." [7] *Another account:* "America, if she fell, would fall like the strong man. She would embrace the pillars of the state, and pull down the constitution along with her. Is this your boasted Peace? Not to sheathe the sword in its scabbard, but to sheathe it in the bowels of your countrymen?" [8]

Debate of May 19, 1772, Walpole's version: "Their thirty-nine Articles were Calvinistical, their Creeds Papistical, and both the Church and Dissenters were every day approaching nearer to Arminianism." [9] *Another account:* "We have a Calvinist creed, a Popish liturgy, and an Arminian clergy." [10]

These passages show that although Walpole did not approach the accuracy and comprehension of a shorthand reporter, he at least correctly rendered the substance of what was said, and in some cases reproduced the exact phrases used by the speaker. In this respect he made a singularly important contribution to historical knowledge, for he is the sole authority for a number of debates and speeches. [11]

On the other hand Walpole frequently showed his bias in his Parliamentary reporting. For example, he made the following summary of part of the debate of November 13, 1755: "Then ensued a variety of the different manners of speaking ill. Potter flimsily; Old Horace Walpole shamelessly; Dr. Hay tritely; George Townshend poorly." [12] As stated this is a criticism of the oratorical abilities of these speakers. But in view of the nature of Walpole's bias, it is impossible to be sure that he was writing in terms of oratory. It may be that he disapproved of what was said, or the passage may be an indirect characterization of the speakers themselves. It is only when he gave a summary of the arguments, without comment, that his reports may be taken at their face value.

Apart from the individual speeches, Walpole's reports of the debates and general Parliamentary proceedings are less satisfactory. In the first place, he was deliberately selective. "The immensity of the debates . . . would, if particularized, fatigue the reader, and swell these cursory memoirs to a tedious compilation." [13] Walpole omitted many debates altogether. He

reported, for example, only five debates in the year 1762.[14] He
left out many speakers in those debates which he reported, as
may be seen by comparing his version of the proceedings of
November 15, 1763, with the report on them made by Grenville
to the king.[15] In other respects Walpole's accounts leave much
to be desired. He made little effort to be exact in matters of
detail. As he explained, "the sense and substance I mean to give,
the forms may be collected by historians, or corrected by
critics." [16] Occasionally he failed to date the debates, or misdated them.[17] His division figures are singularly unreliable, a
circumstance which is unfortunate because the divisions in Committee do not appear regularly in the Parliamentary journals.[18]
At other times Walpole misnamed speakers,[19] telescoped two
debates into one,[20] and made various errors in detail.[21] Although
his reports of the speeches themselves are mainly authentic, his
accounts of Parliamentary proceedings as a whole are far from
reliable.

Walpole's reports of political events outside of Parliament
vary considerably in comprehension and accuracy. The Duke of
Grafton for one believed that he was well informed in the late
1760's, and Grafton was certainly in a position to make a sound
judgment in this respect.[22] On the other hand, in writing a
sustained narrative in his memoirs Walpole often had to describe
events from hearsay. As he once told Lady Ossory, "Everybody
that called on me asserted something or other on *the best
authority,* and every other body that came contradicted his predecessor as positively on as good authority." [23] He was thus
often at the mercy of his informants. As might be expected, he
was prone to believe a disgraceful or humiliating story about
one of his opponents, and he sometimes stated as fact what he
knew to be only probability. Comparison of his version of events
with other contemporary documents reveals a number of factual
errors in his work.

In describing the resignation of the Duke of Devonshire in
October, 1762, Walpole stated that on October 28 the king saw
Devonshire and Newcastle in a chariot together, and suspected
a cabal. Accordingly when Devonshire arrived later that day,
the king refused to see him. Devonshire then resigned his office

of Lord Chamberlain. At the very time that Devonshire presented himself, George III was writing to Lord Bute, "Now was the time," proving that Devonshire's disgrace had been planned. Walpole added his belief that Henry Fox had advised the king in this matter. "Nor could Fox wipe off the suspicion; though, as soon as the affront was known, he had hurried to Devonshire House, and protested his utter ignorance of any such design. The Duke received him coolly, did not pretend to believe him; and his family never forgave it." The next day [October 29] Lord George Cavendish resigned his place, and on November 3 George III struck Devonshire's name from the roster of the Privy Council.[24]

The following inaccuracies appear: First, the king did not see Newcastle and Devonshire together in a chariot. George III stated, "I met the Duke of Devonshire in Hammersmith and the Duke of Newcastle under the terrace in his way to London." [25] That George III related a weaker version of this incident, which enraged him, adds to the credibility of his account. Second, when Devonshire arrived for his audience, the king was not writing to Bute, "Now was the time." Devonshire arrived "a little after one" (according to George III). The king that day wrote three short notes to Bute, at 10:38 A.M., past 3 P.M., and at 5:54 P.M. Aside from the fact that the king was not writing to Bute when Devonshire presented himself (a minor error), none of the three notes to Bute contains the words which Walpole mentioned.[26] Third, Fox did not pay a personal visit to the Duke of Devonshire at Devonshire House to explain his conduct. Instead he wrote to the Duke at Devonshire's seat at Chatsworth on November 2 to express his sorrow and again on November 9 to deny that he had advised striking the Duke's name from the roster of the Privy Council.[27] Fourth, Cavendish resigned on October 31 and not (as Walpole stated) on October 29.[28]

Here Walpole's bias is clearly apparent. Disliking Henry Fox, he insinuated that Fox had intrigued against the Duke of Devonshire, and he probably took pleasure in stating that Fox had been humiliated in a personal interview with the Duke. His errors relative to the meeting of Newcastle and Devonshire, and about the king's correspondence with Bute, may have proceeded from simple misinformation. But of the various versions which Walpole probably heard, he chose a dramatic one, as he did in relation to Fox's humiliation—an indication that his desire to tell an interesting story may have influenced his choice.

A more striking example of Walpole's inaccuracy appears in his verision of the events of May, 1765, when the king tried vainly to rid himself of Grenville's administration. The main features of Walpole's account may be summarized as follows: On May 18 Grenville went to the king and learned that he intended to adjourn Parliament instead of ending the session with a formal prorogation. Grenville asked if he thought of changing the ministry. The king replied "certainly," and asked Grenville who would adjourn the Parliament. Grenville answered, "Whoever your Majesty shall appoint my successor." On May 20 the Duke of Cumberland was sent by the king to Pitt to try to induce Pitt to form an administration, but Pitt refused to accept office. The king then tried unsuccessfully to form a government without Pitt. On May 22 the ministers went to the king, and learning that he would retain them, made three demands: that he promise not to consult Lord Bute again; that he dismiss Mr. Mackenzie (Bute's brother) from the direction of Scottish affairs; and that he appoint Lord Granby as Captain-General of the army. The king replied that he would give his answer that night. In the evening, instead of seeing his ministers, the king sent his answer by the Chancellor: that he agreed to the first two terms, but not to the third. On May 23 the ministers told the king that they accepted the first two conditions, but they added a new demand—the dismissal of Lord Holland from the Pay Office, to which the king agreed.[29]

Walpole's version of these events contains five errors in fact. First, he misdated the interview of Grenville and the king. Grenville saw George III on May 16 and 19. On the 18th the king was at Richmond, and Grenville did not see him at any time on that day.[30] Second, he related as a single interview what actually took place in two conversations between the king and Grenville. The first conversation, on May 16, mainly concerned the question of adjourning. Grenville's reply to the question of who should adjourn the Parliament was not made until May 19.[31]

Third, on the evening of May 22 the king did not send his answer by the Chancellor, but gave it directly and orally to Grenville.[32] Fourth, on the evening of May 22 George III did not agree to both of the first two terms concerning Bute and Mackenzie. At that time he protested against the dismissal of Mackenzie, and it was not until the next morning that he agreed to it.[33] Fifth, on May 23 the ministers did not add as a new demand the dismissal of Lord Holland. This was part of the original five terms, presented on May 22, along with the dismissal of Northumberland from the lord lieutenancy of Ireland, which Walpole did not mention.[34]

At least two of these errors were in part prompted by Walpole's bias. Heartily disliking Grenville, he was predisposed to believe that the king had humiliated his ministers by refusing to give his answer in person. For the same reason, Walpole was prepared to believe that the ministers had not been fair with the king in adding a new demand on May 23 after the first terms had been agreed upon. As for misdating Grenville's first interview, it is noteworthy that he gave the correct date in his letter to Lord Hertford of May 20, 1765. His telescoping the first two interviews of Grenville with the king into one may have been the result of faulty information, but Walpole's version is more dramatic than the events as they happened. It is quite possible that here again his love of a good story may have conditioned his interpretation.

Walpole's account of the events leading to the formation of the first Rockingham administration in July, 1765, is not free from error. The following is a summary of some of the main features of his narrative: On June 20 the Duke of Bedford, accompanied by Grenville, Sandwich, and Halifax, went to the king with a remonstrance, drawn up by Bedford, which took an hour to read. It tended to give the king a month to decide whether to keep his ministers. If he retained them, he must support them with his favor. "Invectives against the Princess were not spared; nor threats of bringing Lord Bute to the block." The king, in anger, did not reply, and merely bowed as a signal for the ministers to retire. George III thereupon opened a negotiation with Pitt, but on Lord Temple's refusing to be part of the proposed new ministry, Pitt declined office. The Duke of Cumberland then opened a negotiation with the Opposition. Accordingly, on June 30 a meeting of 15 Opposition leaders was held at Claremont, Newcastle's seat. It was voted by 10 to 5 to accept office, and despite what Walpole called the "indifferent success" of the meeting, Newcastle reported favorably to Cumberland, and the new ministers "kissed hands" on July 8.[35]

This account contains a number of errors. First, Walpole misdated the interview of Bedford with the king, which took place on June 12, and not June 20. This was probably a clerical error.[36] Second, Walpole stated that Bedford was accompanied by Grenville, Sandwich, and Halifax at that audience. All the available evidence clearly indicates that Bedford was not accompanied by his colleagues.[37] Walpole himself gave a more accurate account in his letter to Mann of June 26, 1765, "The Duke of Bedford, in the name of himself and his three colleagues, prescribed a month to his Majesty . . ." Third, George III did not refuse to reply to Bedford's remonstrance. Although angry, he gave assurances and made an immediate denial of Bedford's allegations about Lord Bute.[38] Fourth, Walpole's account of the meeting at Claremont does not agree in detail with the minute of the meeting prepared by Newcastle. It appears that 18 men were present, and that the vote to accept office was 12 to 6.[39] Fifth, the chief members of the Rockingham administration, and the first to take office, kissed hands on July 10, not July 8.[40]

Walpole's bias is again evident. In stating that the king refused to reply to Bedford's remonstrance, he implied not only that Bedford had been humiliated but that the remonstrance itself was disgraceful. Walpole, of course, disliked Bedford, and was prepared to think ill of him. Again, Walpole's version in his correspondence is more accurate than in the memoirs. It may be noted as well that the presence of four ministers at the audience of June 12 is more dramatic than the presence of Bedford alone, as it makes the remonstrance a ministerial instead of a personal matter, and heightens the coloring of the conflict between the king and his administration.

By way of further illustration, Walpole's account of the formation of the coalition administration of Pitt and Newcastle in June, 1757, while generally accurate, is not free from error.[41] Walpole's errors may have proceeded in part from his bias, for the account clearly put Hardwicke in an unfavorable light. Walpole's feelings for Hardwicke were far from friendly. Walpole made several mistakes in his report on the negotiations between the Court and Bedford in the fall of 1766.[42] This account attacked the conduct of the Duke of Bedford, whom, of course, Walpole disliked. Walpole's version of the resignations of Chatham and Shelburne in 1768 is somewhat garbled.[43] In it Walpole erroneously ascribed Shelburne's fall to intrigues on the part of the Bedford faction. The account also contains insinuations about Chatham's duplicity. Walpole's bias against both Bedford and Chatham is clearly apparent. Finally, Walpole's account of the formation of the second Rockingham administration of 1782 contains four major errors.[44] Much of the distortion here arose from Walpole's dislike of Shelburne and Thurlow, who had prominent parts in the negotiation.

It is manifest that considered as a factual source Walpole's memoirs contain serious imperfections. Often the writing is inexact and misleading. The ever-present emotionalism, expressed in Walpole's various biases, distorts the narrative and creates a false impression. Comparison of Walpole's version of events with other contemporary narratives, mainly those of participants, reveals enough errors, where Walpole can be checked, to cast doubt on those passages which rest on his unsupported testimony. Some of his work, such as his reporting of speeches, is remarkably authentic, and all of it is unusually vivid. But on the whole his memoirs should be used with reserve. The conclusion of Croker is inescapable: "No historian reverent of truth should quote one line from Walpole without a minute investigation of the individual fact, and of the possible *temper* in which Walpole may have related it." [45]

6.

....

Walpole and the Whig Myth

UNTIL RECENTLY the generally accepted opinion of Horace
Walpole has been that he was "a most delicate Italian fop,"[1]
who, "thought, said, and did the silliest things."[2] Isaac Disraeli,
Alexander Chalmers, Lord Holland, and Thackeray have concurred in presenting what amounts to a caricature.[3] Macaulay
thundered, "None but an unhealthy and disorganized mind could
have produced such literary luxuries as the works of Walpole.
He was . . . the most eccentric, the most artificial, the most
fastidious, the most capricious of men. His mind was a bundle
of inconsistent whims and affectations. . . . Serious business was
a trifle to him, and trifles were his serious business."[4] Contempt
for Walpole has percolated even to the level of popular detective
fiction.[5]

To some extent Walpole himself was responsible for the
hostility of his critics. He loved nonsense and despised solemnity.[6]
To Conway he admitted, "I am impenetrably dull in everything
that requires a grain of common sense," and to Lady Ossory he
once commented, "Politics are to me but objects of entertainment
in their turn, like other transient occurrences."[7] In consequence,
one of his critics decided that his serious passages had a "false
ring,"[8] and others followed Macaulay in dismissing his most
sincere pronouncements as mere cant.[9] Leslie Stephen once remarked, "To expect deep and settled political principles from
such a man would be to look for grapes from thorns and figs
from thistles."[10]

More recent interpretations, notably that of his biographer

64

Ketton-Cremer, have stressed Walpole's serious side in an effort to prevent a balanced portrait of his personality.[11] Ketton-Cremer has especially emphasized Walpole's kindliness and moral fervor in trying to save the life of Admiral Byng, who Walpole believed was unjustly condemned to death.[12] It is apparent that Walpole could be deadly serious upon occasion, although like many sensitive people he tended to conceal his emotions behind the shield of his wit. In voicing sober thoughts he was often gauche and self-conscious, or lapsed into nonsense in order to avoid being thought pompous. But the fact that he was not adept in philosophic writing by no means precludes his having a philosophy and has nothing whatsoever to do with his sincerity. To understand Walpole it is well to begin by taking him seriously.

The ideological foundation of Walpole's political thinking was the classic theory of mixed government, as applied to the eighteenth-century English constitution. According to this theory, power in the state was equally divided among three independent bodies, mutually checking one another, so that perfect balance, harmony, and stability resulted. In England the theory had two common expressions: the division of power in the legislature among the king, the House of Lords, and the House of Commons, representing the principles of monarchy, aristocracy, and democracy; and the division of power in the state among the king, the Parliament, and the courts, representing the executive, legislative, and judicial aspects of government.[13] Promulgated by Plato and Aristotle and formulated by Polybius, this theory was repeated by Cicero and by Machiavelli, and was known to Elizabethan scholars, but it first attained currency in England during the Civil Wars of the seventeenth century as an argument against the absolutist pretensions of the Stuart kings. After the Revolution of 1688 it found wide acceptance. In constitutional discussions the theory became commonplace, chiefly as an Opposition argument against Crown influence in Parliament, but also as a ministerial argument for the status quo. Across the Atlantic the theory became a vital force in the writing of the American constitution.[14]

Such a theory was particularly attractive to thinkers of

the Enlightenment, mainly because it was simple and orderly. Starting with the Newtonian concept of a universe governed by calculable mathematical principles, the philosophers of the eighteenth century tried to find comparable laws within the body politic. The theory of balanced government seemed "natural," that is, metaphysically valid, because harmony in the political microcosm appeared to be a counterpart of Divine Order in the macrocosm.[15]

The psychological presupposition underlying the theory was distrust of human nature. As Walpole expressed it, "Knowing a little of human nature, as I have lived to do, and how unfit one man or all are to be trusted with unlimited power . . . I must admire our own constitution." [16] In strictly political terminology, this distrust became fear of each of the three classic forms of government in its pure and unmixed form. In 1781 MacDonald told the House of Commons, "Democracy was as much to be avoided as monarchy, or aristocracy." [17] Slightly earlier a pamphleteer remarked, "The people are better in any hands than their own, and the cruellest tyrant is a miracle of mercy when compared with the people set free from all restraint, and let loose one upon another." [18] Such expressions were typical.[19] In general the Whig aristocracy, fearful alike of absolutism and of democracy, formulated its concept of good government as delicately poised somewhere in between. By mid century the Whigs were thinking in terms of Parliamentary or aristocratic supremacy instead of the contractual resistence theories which had justified the Revolution of 1688.[20]

Walpole has stated the theory of mixed government in terms of the fears currently expressed by the ruling class. "The legislature consists of the three branches of King, Lords, and Commons. Together they form our invaluable constitution, and each is a check on the other two. But it must be remembered, at the same time, that while any two are checking, the third is naturally aiming at extending and aggrandizing its power. The House of Commons has not seldom made this attempt, like the rest. The Lords, as a permanent and as a proud body, more constantly aim at it; the Crown always." [21]

During his lifetime Walpole had occasion to change his mind

several times as to which element in the tri-partite state was the most dangerous. In his early years, as Becker has observed, Walpole appears to have been most apprehensive of the aristocracy, but until the outbreak of the American Revolution, "he had no settled convictions. . . . It was now the Crown, now the aristocracy, and now the mob that he feared."[22] After 1775 Walpole tended to concentrate his fear on the Crown and on the people. "Republics veer towards aristocracy or democracy, and often end in a single tyrant,—not that nobles are not tyrants. For the people, they are not capable of government, and do more harm in an hour, when heated by popular incendiaries than a king can do in a year."[23] A few years later Walpole's emphasis shifted. "Silly people are apt to say, I had rather be governed by an absolute monarch, than by the mob—but no country is governed by the mob. In mere democratic government, a sort of government that never can exist long, the multitude may do many absurd and many unjust things—but what is called the mob in any regal country, however limited the Crown, is an accidental, and a very transient tumult, and never did last above a few days—whereas the power of an absolute monarch is permanent."[24] In short, he believed the Crown to be more efficient than the people, and therefore a greater menace to the state. As he declared in his earliest memoirs, "By all observations I have made on the course of this world and its affairs, it appears to me, that the tendency of governments has been to universal monarchy."[25] In true Whig fashion he expressed preference for "most limited monarchy" or "the shadow of monarchy," and once went so far as to speak of "the least bad of all murders, that of a king."[26]

Macaulay took particular exception to this last comment, and tried to show that Walpole had apostatized his political principles by professing republicanism in his youth and becoming a "fanatical royalist" in his old age, in reaction to the French Revolution.[27] Macaulay's charge is unfair. As Mary Berry correctly observed, "In politics, he was what he professed to be, a *Whig*, in the sense which that denomination bore in his younger days,—*never* a republican."[28] Whenever Walpole came to define his so-called republican tendencies, he qualified them so carefully that they end in becoming something quite different. "My reflections led me early towards, I cannot quite say republicanism, but to most limited monarchy. . . . Yet republicanism, as it tends to promote liberty, and patriotism as far as it tends to preserve or restore it, are still godlike principles. A republican who should be mad, should be execrable enough to endeavor to imbrue his country in blood merely to remove the name of a monarch, deserves to excite horror." [29]

This qualification follows the basic pattern of Walpole's political philosophy. It has been observed that he could never forget that he was the son of an earl.[30] Aristocratic and fastidious, he recoiled at the prospect of class levelling. "Being by my station an aristocrat," he wrote candidly, "I cannot wish to be swept into the common sewers." [31] Such a declaration is hardly the comment of a republican. Further, Walpole's horror at the French Revolution was not a denial of his Whiggism. To the contrary it was an affirmation of his political faith, as he saw the entire fabric of the balanced constitution endangered by the forces of democracy. His decision was unwavering. "I have lived long enough to see the King, Lords, Commons, preponderate at different periods. . . . The first power has undoubtedly of late years been the heaviest; but that fourth power, that within these two years has started out of the earth like the black cloud in the *Arabian Nights,* and which dispersing, disclosed an infernal Afrite—that power does not tend to balance, but overturn all three." [32] Conservatism of this order placed Walpole in the right, or Rockingham-Portland wing of the Whigs, who refused to countenance any reform in the fundamental structure of the balanced constitution.[33] "I love the constitution I am used to," he wrote to Mann, "and wish to leave it behind me." [34] Constitutional innovations in general, and Parliamentary reform in particular, filled him with dismay. "It would be wise," he wrote, "to restore the constitution before we try experiments on it." [35] Reforms such as annual elections, he decided, "would soon annihilate the dignity of Parliament, or grow such a nuisance that very likely prerogative would be adopted as a counterpoison." [36] For much the same reason that he abominated reformers, Walpole despised Tories. "A Whig may be a fool," he once declared, "A Tory must be so. . . . A Tory attaining power hurries to establish despotism: the honor, the trade, the wealth, the peace of the nation, all are little to him in comparison of the despotic will of his master." [37] In terms of his basic ideology, Tories and reformers alike, as they leaned towards absolutism or democracy, tended to overthrow the balance of the constitution, and were in consequence dangerous persons.

It is apparent that Walpole's political principles, far from being capricious, remained remarkably consistent. Although there were several changes in emphasis, his philosophical postulates did not change. The reason for this consistency is not far to seek. Walpole's political principles were articles of faith, which he accepted on the level of religious belief. He even went so far as to declare, "I would have an exposition of our triformed constitution drawn up . . . and *then reduced to a corollary of implicit faith*. I would have all schools, seminaries, colleges, universities, obliged to inculcate this creed into all the youth committed to their care." [38] It was in this quasi-religious frame of mind that Walpole approached contemporary political problems.

Walpole's attitude did not lead to objective analysis, and it is only to be expected that he misinterpreted many political phenomena. In company with a number of his contemporaries, he made a series of charges against George III which, taken together, constitute an invidious tradition. Bolstered by the authority of not a few respectable historians, this tradition has achieved, until recently, the status of orthodox interpretation. In reality it is little more than a political fantasy, which may be termed the Whig myth, that is, a collection of beliefs about George III which the Whigs expressed. As will appear, not one of the beliefs in the Whig myth was based on fact, and the myth itself survived largely as a symbolic expression of political self-righteousness and as a convenient means of maligning all non-Whigs.

Walpole's allegations about George III may be summarized as follows: (1) George III was educated by Jacobites and Tories, who taught him that he must free himself from the aristocratic Whig faction which had oppressed George II. (2) George III used "secret influence" and a hidden cabal around the throne, as well as a corps of King's friends in Parliament, to undermine the authority of his ministers. (3) George III attempted to revive prerogative and to overthrow the established constitution.

Until the period of the American Revolution, Walpole was generally pleased with George III. At his accession Walpole commented that the king "behaved with the greatest propriety, dignity, and decency." [39] In three successive letters to Mann he spoke of the king as "amiable." [40] Five years later his view was still sympathetic. "Prerogative—alack! he is grown so tame, that, as you said of our earthquake, you may stroke him. George the Third is the true successor of George the Second, and inherits all his grandfather's humiliations." [41] In 1770 Walpole viewed the king as "much to be pitied; abandoned where he had most confidence, and attacked on every other side." [42] That same year he attended the king's levee, although in the past he had prided himself on his aloofness to the court. [43]

It was not until the outbreak of the American Revolution in 1775 that his sympathy for George III soured into acrimony. In September of that year he exclaimed to Mann, "Oh, mad, mad England! What frenzy, to throw away its treasures . . . that its prince may be arbitrary lord of boundless deserts in America." [44] Henceforth Walpole's aversion to George III was implacable. In *Last Journals* he pictured the king as obstinate without courage and possessed of "infinite hypocrisy," [45] and in the "Journal 1783–91" his hostility continued to be unremitting. Walpole's ultimate characterization of George III was bitter in the extreme. "There were but four leading characteristics in the King's composition. He was unfeeling, insincere, cunning and trifling. Nature had given him the first quality, and the last. His mother had taught him the second, and practise the third. . . . His constancy to the Queen was owing to his pride, suspicion, and a very governable constitution, not to affection for her. . . . His extreme temperence was no more a virtue than his chastity. The malignant humor in his blood could only be kept down by the abstemiousness of a hermit." [46] Walpole was equally severe on the king's public life. "It is obvious that every

disgrace and misfortune that has fallen on the King has proceeded from only those ministers whom he himself approved.
By removing Lord Chatham, Lord Bute was enabled to strike
up the shameful Peace of Paris, which saved France and enabled
her to support the Americans. By the compliance of Lord North,
war was made on America. By the courtly treachery of Lord
Shelburne, the American royalists were abandoned; and by Mr.
Pitt's ambition, Mr. Fox's India bill was prevented." [47] "Thus
did he purchase triumph by the grossest duplicity and barter the
honor of a gentleman to display the power of a king." [48] Antipathy to George III became one of the ruling passions of Walpole's
later years and profoundly influenced his political interpretations in his memoirs and journals.

In 1772 Walpole finished the draft of his *Memoirs of George
III*, but he transcribed them in 1775, and made extensive re-
visions and additions, particularly to the first and fourth volumes
(as printed) as late as 1784.[49] In consequence these memoirs
contain Walpole's after-thoughts and hindsight, especially as
he projected his later hostility to George III back to periods
where his correspondence shows him to have been sympathetic
to the king.[50] In the fourth volume he included an analysis of
Burke's *Thoughts on the Cause of the Present Discontents*, in
a long passage which was in part composed in 1784, when
Walpole had turned against the king.[51] This pamphlet, published
in April, 1770, as a political manifesto of the Rockingham
Whigs, was one of the critical catalysts in the formation of the
Whig myth.[52]

Burke attacked the augmented power of the Crown, oper-
ating, so he charged, by a system of double cabinets. He argued
that a cabal in the secret confidence of the king and supported
in Parliament by the King's friends, undermined the ostensible
ministers of state. This system, so Burke contended, resulted
from a concerted plot, founded in the supposition that George II
had been oppressed by his ministers, to gain for the present
king the unrestricted exercise of the royal power, independent
of ministerial or Parliamentary controls. The first step, Burke
asserted, was the elevation of Bute to the head of the government, but this expedient was soon abandoned. The Crown then

fomented dissension in order to break down party loyalties, and the King's friends tried to subvert the right of freedom of election (in Wilkes' case) in order to separate members of Parliament from their constituents. Such a system, Burke argued, allowed the Crown to use its power independently of the will of the people, as expressed in Parliament. Regarding correctives, Burke rejected both the proposal of more frequent elections and the exclusion of placemen from Parliament. Instead he advocated a closer connection between members and constituents, and a greater party solidarity within Parliament itself. He ended on a characteristic Whig note, that unless such reforms were made, civil violence or despotism would inevitably result.

Walpole's reaction to Burke's pamphlet as expressed in his *Memoirs of George III* was not entirely favorable. He made three criticisms which probably reflected his opinions before 1775: first, that Burke had alienated "the popular party" by declaring against triennial Parliaments and place bills; and second, that Burke was "absurd" in exonerating Bute from present influence. Walpole's third criticism was that in pleading for party unity Burke ignored the importance of conscience.[53] Here Walpole saw an attack on the independent conduct of his cousin General Conway.

Walpole's fourth criticism, that Burke had not found the real source of the discontents, appears to reflect his attitude in 1784, when his hostility to George III had matured. Walpole contended that the root of the present trouble lay in the last reign. Two main hypotheses follow: "that the Pelhams, Hardwicke, and their friends were an aristocratic faction; that they insulted and provoked the Crown and Royal family, and raised digusts in them against the Whig party, at the same time planting the rankest Tories about the successor and his mother, forcing them to throw themselves into the arms of even Jacobites."[54]

Walpole then marshalled evidence in support of his contentions. He began by citing a number of instances as proof that the Pelhams were an "aristocratic faction": in 1746 they deserted Lord Granville and forced George II to take them back as ministers against his will; the Pelhams passed the Marriage Act to protect the wealth of the nobility; Mansfield opposed the extension of habeas corpus; and Byng's "murder" resulted from Anson's "negligence" and Newcastle's "panic." [55]

Having established his first point to his own satisfaction, Walpole turned to the education of George III. "So blinded were the Pelhams by their own ambition, that they furnished the Princess with men whose abilities were best suited to inspire arbitrary notions into her son, and to instruct him how to get rid of his tyrants, and establish a despotism. . . . On the death of the late King, the Princess, Lord Bute, and their junto, provoked, as I have said, by the great Whig Lords, inclined to the Tories and by the counsels of Bolingbroke, Mansfield, and Stone, and disposed by the love of power to rise above the constitution, had one capital view—the restoration of prerogative." [56]

At this point, his acceptance of the foundation of the Whig myth being virtually complete, Walpole recalled his own part in attacking George III's education. In 1752 he had circulated an anonymous memorial, which stated that the heir apparent was being educated in reactionary and despotic principles. Largely as a result of this memorial,[57] charges of Jacobitism were brought against the Prince's preceptors, Andrew Stone and Murray (later Lord Mansfield). In February, 1753, a Committee in Council investigated the matter and acquitted the defendants; in March, the House of Lords reviewed the evidence and ruled that the accusations were groundless. But in revising his *Memoirs of George III* Walpole re-affirmed his earlier accusations and stated that the Committee in Council and the House of Lords had been negligent in their examination of the charges.[58] Ultimately the reactionary education of George III became an integral part of Walpole's political interpretation of the reign. "The King," he wrote, "it was given out, *would* be King—would *not* be dictated to by his ministers, as his grandfather had been." [59] Walpole also mentioned "the ruling principle of the reign, which had been by breaking and dividing all parties, to draw attention and dependence only to the King himself." [60] In assessing Walpole's contribution to the Whig myth, it is significant that he made his accusations against Stone and Murray almost twenty years before the appearance of Burke's pamphlet.

The charge that George III was educated in reactionary

principles gained sufficient currency, or was politically dangerous
enough, to merit a formal investigation in 1753, and as opposition
to George III grew, it became widely believed. Junius in his
celebrated letter to the king spoke of the "pernicious lessons
you received in your youth," and John Nicholls reported that
the Princess Dowager repeatedly admonished her son, "George,
be King." [61] Shelburne placed the blame on Bute for representing
the Whigs to the young Prince "as having from a levelling republican party degenerated into an aristocratical faction, who kept
his grandfather in chains." [62] Grafton repeated the substance
of these charges without naming the persons responsible.[63] And
following the same line of thought, the Duke of Portland declared, "The characteristic feature of the present reign has
been . . . to annihilate, if possible, the Whig party." [64]

Walpole was an enthusiastic believer in the second main
postulate of the Whig myth, that George III used "secret influence," a hidden cabal, and a corps of Kings friends to undermine
the authority of his ministers. "Not one of his various ministers,"
Walpole asserted, "ever had his perfect confidence, and though
he prated eternally and often impudently, he always reserved
his chief secrets to himself." [65] Repeatedly Walpole stated his
belief that Bute gave secret advice to the king long after his
public resignation in 1763.[66] When, in 1767, Lord Holland
assured him that Bute had not seen the king alone for two years,
Walpole flatly refused to believe him.[67] Although he admitted
that he had changed his mind several times as to the duration of
Bute's secret influence, Walpole ultimately came to believe that
the king had consulted Bute as late as 1783.[68] At any event, in
Charles Jenkinson, "able, shrewd, timid, cautious and dark,"
Walpole saw Bute's successor as the "director or agent of all
his Majesty's secret counsels." [69] He accused Mansfield of offering
secret advice as well.[70] His reaction to the fall of the Fox-North
coalition in 1783 was typical. "The secret influence was no longer
secret; the Duke of Portland's administration was openly overturned by the exertion of that influence." [71] As for the corps of
King's friends mentioned by Burke, Walpole for the most part
contented himself with stigmatizing court followers as the crea-
tures or tools of Lord Bute, in much the same way that he had

attempted to discredit his father's opponents by calling them Jacobites.[72]

The charge that George III used secret influence to undermine his ministers became a warcry of the Opposition. In the House of Lords Effingham complained of such influence, and Rockingham spoke of "unconstitutional control and advice." [73] In the House of Commons Fletcher Norton and Thomas Pitt both declared that secret influence was more dangerous than an open exercise of the prerogative, and Fox did not hesitate to accuse Jenkinson of giving secret advice to the king.[74] The cry was taken up in popular pamphlets: "The system of secret and personal influence tends to subvert the constitution." [75] "The secret abettors of that pernicious system have been laboring to establish their power on the ruins of every maxim of constitutional government." [76] Along with the charge of secret influence came the related allegation that there existed a hidden cabal. Lord Chesterfield told his son, "You seem not to know the character of the Queen. . . . The King loves her as a woman; but I verily believe, has never yet spoken one word about business; that is reserved entirely for the nocturnal conferences with the Princess of Wales and Lord Bute." [77] Wraxall has left an extended description of the popularity of this belief.[78] Walpole's contemporaries believed, with him, that not only Jenkinson but also Mansfield offered secret advice to the king, and Junius was active in attacking court supporters in Parliament as the King's friends.[79]

Walpole was a fervent upholder of the third premise in the Whig myth, that George III attempted to revive prerogative and to overthrow the established constitution. He wrote in his *Memoirs of George III:* "The contradictions which the King suffered in his ill-advised measures, riveted in him a thirst of delivering himself from control, and to be above control he must be absolute. Thus on the innate desire of unbounded power in all princes, was engrafted a hate to the freedom of the subject, and therefore, whether the King set out with a plan of extending his prerogative, or adopted it, his subsequent measures, as often as he had an opportunity of directing them, tended to the sole object of acting by his own will." [80] In *Last Journals* Walpole elaborated his concept: "I had long dreaded lest success or despair should infuse resolution enough into the King to endeavor to establish absolute power by the army. Had the conquest of America been achieved, I have not the slightest doubt but a triumphant army, returned from subduing the King's enemies, and stigmatized by the Americans as Tories, would have been unbounded, being ready to make war on all called Whigs." [81] In the "Journal 1783–91" Walpole repeated his former assertion in even stronger terms: "General Conway owned to me that he now did believe what I had long tried to persuade him, that the King from the beginning had meant to be absolute, and at last to govern by the army, which I had long observed him to court, and fill with Scots, and late Jacobites and high Tories." [82]

For the most part Walpole's contemporaries expressed their opposition to George III in milder language, doubtless because it was not prudent to make an open assertion that the king was a tyrant. Nevertheless, in 1780 in the House of Lords Rockingham spoke of the "principles of despotism, which seemed to pervade all the acts of the present reign," and in the House of Commons in 1781 Burgoyne remarked on "the strides of the Crown towards absolute power." [83] Burke, Fox, and the Duke of Richmond publicly inveighed against the possible despotic consequences of the king's control of the army. [84] But few Englishmen went as far as the Americans in the Declaration of Independence: "The history of the present King of Great Britain is a history of repeated injuries and usurpations, all having, in direct object, the establishment of an absolute tyranny over these states."

In general the Opposition distinguished between the king's prerogative and his influence. Blackstone had observed in his *Commentaries* (1765): "The Crown has, gradually and imperceptibly, gained almost as much in influence as it has apparently lost in prerogative," and Burke in his *Thoughts on the Cause of the Present Discontents* had commented, "The power of the Crown, almost dead and rotten as prerogative, has grown up anew, with much more strength, and far less odium, under the name of influence." [85] Even Junius acquitted the king of despotic inclinations and emphasized royal influence instead of royal prerogative.[86] The distinction between prerogative and influence was widely drawn in Parliament and in popular tracts,[87] and on April 6, 1780, the House of Commons passed Dunning's famous resolution, "that the influence of the Crown has increased, is increasing, and ought to be diminished."

It is clear that the term "influence" was used in its purely political connotation, to mean "the accumulation of Parliamentary votes by patronage in the control of ministers."[88] Or, as Martin told the House of Commons during the debate on Dunning's resolution, "the present influence of the Crown was founded in corruption."[89] Influence, then, was royal patronage, and the movement for economical reform, sponsored by the Rockingham Whigs in 1780–2, was an attempt to curtail the revenues of the Crown in order to decrease the king's weight in Parliament.[90] A pamphleteer asserted, "The establishment of immediate and personal influence has been the leading principle during the whole of the present reign,"[91] and a second added, "That such an influence existing, may destroy the equilibrium of our constitution, is self-evident."[92] The Yorkshire and other petitioners for economical reform went further, stating, "The Crown has acquired a great and unconstitutional influence, which if not checked may soon prove fatal to the liberties of the country."[93]

Walpole has recorded his belief in an ancillary expression of the Whig myth, namely that the Princess Dowager, George III's mother, was Bute's mistress. His most detailed statement of this notion occurs in the *Memoirs of George II* in a passage which was in part censored by Lord Holland in his capacity as editor: [94] "It had already been whispered that the assiduity of Lord Bute at Leicester House, and his still more frequent attendance in the gradens at Kew and Carlton House were less addressed to the Prince than to his mother. The eagerness of the pages of the backstairs to let her know whenever Lord Bute arrived, a mellowness in her German accent as often as she spoke to him and that was often and long, and a more than usual swimmingness in her eyes, contributed to dispell the ideas that had been conceived of the rigor of her widowhood. On the other hand, the favored personage seemed by no means desirous of concealing his conquest. . . . Her eyes had often twinkled intelligibly enough at her countryman Prince Lobkowitz; yet perhaps she had never passed the critical barrier, if her simple husband, when he took up the character of the regent's gallantry, had not forced an air of intrigue even upon his wife." Elsewhere Walpole referred to Bute as "the Princess's minion" or as "her silly paramour." [95] Although once he admitted that their intimacy could not be proved,[96] he is reported to have declared, "I am as much convinced of an amorous connection . . . as if I had seen them together." [97]

The supposedly adulterous relations of Bute and the Princess became common scandal. Bute was reputed to be the father of her last child, Caroline Matilda, born over four months after the death of Frederick, Prince of Wales.[98] Lord Waldegrave, who was prominent in the Leicester-House circle, alluded to the scandal without denying it, and George III was infuriated when he heard the gossip about Bute and his mother four years before he came to the throne.[99] Wilkes made much of this gossip in his notorious *Essay on Women* and in the *North Briton,* and it has been suggested that much of George III's hostility toward Wilkes proceeded from Wilkes' reflections on his mother.[100] In the House of Commons Calvert boldly alluded to the scandal, as did Junius in his letter to the king.[101] The scandal was the subject of many satirical prints of the period, and the mob delighted in calling attention to it by burning symbolically a jack-boot (a pun on Bute's name) and a petticoat.[102]

In addition to the Whig myth there was a counteractive, which might be called the Tory myth. The crux of the Tory argument was that an aristocratic faction had deprived the king of his fair share of power in the tri-partite constitution, and, as a pamphleteer expressed it, "Formidable, therefore, as this [royal] influence may appear, it is now, by many, thought indispensably necessary to give the Crown its due weight in the state." [103] Goldsmith urged support of the Crown, as "that sacred power that has for some years been every day declining, and losing its due share of influence," and in 1763 Sir John Philipps begged George III not to become "a King in shackles" like his grandfather.[104] In a tract entitled *Seasonable Hints from an Honest Man,* Englishmen were urged to resist "the dark and arbitrary influence of aristocracy" and were exhorted "to support the throne and constitution against ministerial insolence, and corrupt administration." [105] Mrs. Catherine Macaulay, in a tract published in 1770, stated that Burke had overrated the danger of royal influence and had attempted "to mislead the people on the subject of the more complicated and specious, though no less dangerous maneuvers of aristocratic faction." [106] Burges applied this view to the defeat of Fox's India bills in December, 1783: "The House of Lords, however, approved themselves the true and faithful supporters of the Crown and constitution. They rejected the bill and emancipated the Sovereign from bondage to a desperate and unscrupulous faction." [107] In 1796 the diarist Farington repeated the Tory argument: "The Portlands, Cavendishes, Bedfords, Fitzwilliams etc. hold themselves distinct from the nobility in general in a political respect. Having contributed to the establishment of the present family on the throne, they claim a sort of right to extraordinary power under it. The present King has resisted with sagacity, and success, their united endeavors." [108] This argument, as articulated in Dodington's *Diary* (1784) and given classic expression in John Adolphus' *History* (1802), provided until the middle of the nineteenth century the main interpretation of the early years of George III's reign.[109]

Critical examination of the three basic premises in the Whig myth, and of the premise in the Tory counter-myth, reveals that they do not rest upon valid factual evidence. Recent research has exploded the notion that George III was educated by Tories and Jacobites in reactionary principles. Re-examination of the charges against the Prince's preceptors, Stone and Murray, leads to the conclusion that these men were unjustly, and possibly maliciously, accused.[110] A study of George III's correspondence with Bute in the years 1756–66 reveals that far from having absorbed reactionary principles the young Prince was in fact nourished on a series of quite harmless "constitutional platitudes." [111] Had Walpole and the Whigs had opportunity of examining George III's highly idealistic constitutional pronouncements, they might have been more cautious in their charges that the Prince had been educated in reactionary political beliefs.

Moreover, George III's expressed wish to emancipate himself from a factious oligarchy was not an innovation. George II had complained that he was "under the domination of an aristocracy," and he once remarked to Hardwicke that "Ministers are the Kings in this country." [112] To free the Crown from the tyranny of its ministers was a standard constitutional fiction of eighteenth-century English heirs-apparent to the throne when they supported an opposition to the government.[113] In 1711 Swift commented that "the Queen was no longer able to bear the tyranny and insolence of those ungrateful servants," and in opposition to Robert Walpole's administration Bolingbroke observed, "They who could never brook a regal, will have the merit of saving their country from a ministerial tyranny." [114] Robert Walpole himself used this argument when he was leader of a Leicester-House opposition, as Burke was to revive it to champion the pretensions of Carlton House against George III and the younger Pitt.[115] That George III and Bute frequently inveighed against the oppression of an aristocratic faction is well established.[116] To the Whigs their complaint was proof of the king's reactionary education, and to the Tories it was a useful blast against the Whigs. But in either case the argument was based on so transparent a fiction that it cannot be taken at its face value. Recent research has established that George II's alleged bondage in the hands of an oligarchy was a legend without foundation in fact.[117]

The second premise in the Whig myth, dealing with secret influence, double cabinets, and the King's friends, rests upon equally flimsy evidence. Lord North publicly denied that secret influence had existed while he was head of the government.[118] Bute likewise exculpated himself, as did the king and Jenkinson.[119] So far, at least, as Bute is concerned, there is no valid evidence to indicate that he saw the king alone, or advised him on political matters, after 1766, and there is evidence that George III himself took the initiative in preventing Bute from meddling in affairs of state.[120]

Likewise there is no truth in Burke's charge that George III ruled by a system of double cabinets.[121] In reality Burke did little more than revive the familiar political wail against a secret cabinet council or cabal, a complaint often voiced in the days of William III and Anne, as an echo of the "Cabal" in Charles II's time, and thoroughly hackneyed when it appeared in the *Craftsman* in 1730 as a charge against Robert Walpole.[122]

As for the King's friends, the term was known in the reign of George II at least as early as 1734, just as there were "Queen's servants" under Anne.[123] In this connection the historian Earl Stanhope has made a penetrating observation: "Several of these were men in office, many more were independent members of Parliament."[124] Namier's researches indicate that many of the King's friends or "Treasury Jesuits" were, as Stanhope suggested, in actuality ambitious civil servants, who supported every administration in its turn, because, as any place which could be held along with a seat in Parliament was in practise reserved for an M.P., they had to remain in Parliament in order to continue in the government service.[125] It appears also that many country gentlemen were called Tories or King's friends, merely because they refused to ally themselves with any faction or group in Parliament.[126] Lord Hervey expressed devotion to George II in 1742 in terms which twenty years later would have earned for him the sobriquet of a King's friend. "I belong to no class, faction or party; have no attachment but to your service; no connection but to your interest and inclination; belong to you and no other, and am attacked and pursued for no other reason."[127]

The third allegation in the Whig myth, that George III wished to revive prerogative and overturn the established constitution, also has no foundation in fact. Recent historians are for the most part unanimous in rejecting this allegation.[128] Lord North frequently declared that the king would live on bread and water to preserve the constitution.[129] So far from taking the Tory view that the Crown should deal with the American colonies, George III upheld the supremacy of Parliament. "I am fighting the battle of the legislature," he declared, "therefore have a right to expect an almost unanimous support."[130] One may go beyond Guttridge's remark that "the King had stolen

Whig thunder," [131] and conclude that in 1775 George III was the first Whig in the kingdom.

As for "influence," George III merely made full use of the system of patronage which had been built up by Robert Walpole and the Pelhams.[132] Defenders of the king argued correctly that royal influence was an essential ingredient in the machinery of state. Both publicly and in private Richard Rigby maintained that "without influence and what is called undue influence too, this government could not subsist." [133] Dr. Johnson shared Rigby's view.[134] The legal historian Sir William Holdsworth has stated that a "link of influence" was in practise necessary to insure cooperation between the three theoretically separate bodies in the tri-partite constitution.[135] In short, George III's use of "influence" was neither excessive nor unusual. What the Rockingham Whigs wished to accomplish in their campaign for economical reform, when the cry of "undue influence" reached its peak, was to deprive the Crown of exclusively royal patronage, while leaving untouched the patronage regularly dispensed by the Crown's ministers, for the Rockingham Whigs had no wish to cripple their own operations when in future, so they hoped, they should be called upon to form an administration.[136]

George III was stubborn and often tactless. His striking the name of the Duke of Devonshire from the roster of the Privy Council in 1762 was both ungracious and unwise. It has been observed that had he pardoned Wilkes he would have been the most popular English monarch since Charles II.[137] Instead he was unpopular, at least during the first twenty-three years of his reign, to the point of being subjected to abuse by the mob.[138] Until 1783 there was no adult heir-apparent, around whom a systematic opposition could crystalize.[139] In addition, the unwritten constitution left still unsettled the vexing question of the extent to which a royal minister or cabinet should have support in the Parliament.[140] The confusions and antagonisms of the early years of his reign may, then, be satisfactorily explained without resorting to the Whig hypothesis that George III made undue and abnormal use of "influence."

It remains to dispose of the ancillary expression of the Whig myth that the Princess Dowager was Bute's mistress. Walpole himself admitted that there was no proof behind the charge,[141] and while the question will probably never be satisfactorily settled, there are two bodies of evidence which tend strongly to discredit the scandal. First, a study of George III's correspondence with Bute suggests that it was not the Princess but her eldest son who was infatuated with Lord Bute.[142] Second, a passage in Walpole's *Memoirs of George II*, deleted by Lord Holland, actually indicates in its implications that the Princess and Bute were not lovers.[143] Moreover, some of Walpole's well-informed contemporaries refused to believe that they were.[144]

It is evident, then, that the Whig myth and the Tory counter-myth do not rest upon a firm foundation of fact. George III was not educated by Jacobites and Tories in reactionary principles, and his expressed determination to be free of ministerial tyranny was little more than a transparent fiction. George III made occasional use of irresponsible advisers, but he did not adhere to a concerted system of "secret influence" and "double cabinets" in any way approaching the extent alleged by the Whigs. The so-called corps of King's friends was largely a body of permanent civil servants and independent country gentlemen who had professed non-partisan devotion to the Crown in the time of George II. George III did not attempt to augment prerogative, and he had no wish to overturn the established constitution. His use of patronage in the machinery of state was a normal and necessary constitutional practise, exercised in his case without tact and in the absence of an adult heir-apparent before 1783. The ancillary expression of the Whig myth, relative to Bute and the Princess, was not based on valid proof, and there exists evidence which tends to contradict it. As for the Tory counter-myth, that George II and George III were victims of oppression by an aristocratic faction, that notion also was a constitutional fiction. In short, the entire fabric of this invidious tradition is pure political folklore.

The question naturally arises, why did Walpole and his contemporaries believe, or profess to believe, such obvious nonsense? One explanation may be found in the nature of a myth *per se*. In its broadest sense myth achieves the stature of metaphysics, and arises from, as Cassirer has stated, "the desire of human nature to come to terms with reality, to live in an ordered universe, and to overcome the chaotic state in which things and thoughts have not yet assumed a definite shape and structure." The inner necessity to find unity in life is the universal motive behind all myth-making, and the myth itself, as a symbolic explanation of the macrocosm, is emotional in origin, for the intellect merely makes cogent the image which the emotion evokes. Ultimately myth becomes the "objectification of man's social experience" and "the art of expressing, and that means of organizing, his most deeply rooted instincts, his hopes and fears." [145] In view of the foregoing, it appears entirely natural that Walpole and his contemporaries should have constructed a political mythology about George III. The Whig myth offered to them a symbolic explanation of the reign; it objectified their fears of despotism; and it kept alive their hopes for a Whig-controlled state.

From a somewhat different point of view, a political tradition, such as the Whig myth, may be viewed as a moral rather than as a metaphysical entity. It has been said that "A tradition is not a mere observed fact like an existing custom, nor a story that exhausts its significance in being told; it is an idea which expresses a value judgment. A certain way of acting is regarded as right; a certain order or arrangement is held desirable. The maintenance of the tradition is the assertion of this judgment." [146] Walpole and his contemporaries lived in an intellectual climate which was saturated with moral sentiments. They took pleasure in passing judgment, in ethical terms, upon their political opponents, for the very human reason that such criticism was self-praise in reverse. As Walpole said, "I like to give my opinion on what I have seen . . . I like to keep up the thread of my observations." [147] Disapproving of George III for personal or abstract reasons, Walpole and his contemporaries, either deliberately (as seems to have been the case with Burke) or unconsciously (as appears probable in Walpole's case) fabricated a tissue of supposedly factual statements, as an embodiment of their moral indignation. So long as belief, or profession of belief, in their delusions appeared useful for propaganda purposes, or pleasurable for purposes of self-gratification, they persisted in repeating the various allegations of the myth.

Another reason for the continuing expression of the myth lies in the prevalence in the eighteenth century of intellectual fictions, which were largely borrowed in spirit from the law or from constitutional apologetics. One such fiction was the idea of an original compact between the king and the people. Another was the polite hypocrisy that the king can do no wrong. It was customary to argue in terms of such euphemisms and abstractions, possibly as a phase of oratorical eloquence, instead of using starkly realistic language. Thus, as has been suggested,[148] an attack on the king's secret advisers was a camouflaged attack upon the king himself. The same sort of indirection pervades the attacks on the "reactionaries" held responsible for the education of the king. In each case, the king himself remained ostensibly blameless, but surrounded by evil men. Walpole himself used the verbal paraphernalia of indirection when his remarks were public or liable to be made public, and it is only in his memoirs, written in secret, that he cut through the web of fiction and made an attack direct on the king.

The formulation of the myth illustrates once again the violence inherent in eighteenth-century English political life. The scandal about Bute and the Princess persisted largely because it was politically effective. The entire myth proper, with its implications of a deep seated and sinister plot, and its evil protagonists, Bute, Jenkinson, Mansfield, the Princess, and the king, partakes of the character of melodrama, quite in keeping with the tone of Ciceronian inventive which pervaded the oratory of the Houses of Parliament. It represents, moreover, the eighteenth-century habit of proving one's opponent wrong by proving that he was wicked.

One further aspect of the myth deserves attention, that of secrecy: the cabal exerted secret influence on the king, and the king used arcane devices to undermine his ministers; Bute, the Princess, and George III met by stealth at night; Jenkinson carried furtive messages; and the king plotted behind the scenes to overthrow the constitution with military force. This aspect of the myth certainly enhanced its dramatic quality, but it also reflected the commonly held eighteenth-century belief that secret causes often produced great events. The element of secrecy had the double-barreled appeal of being not only dramatic but decidedly plausible.

Later historians accepted the myths for somewhat different reasons. Americans such as Bancroft were eager to believe ill of George III in order to justify the American Revolution.[149] Among English historians the Tory myth, that George III was trying to emancipate himself from a powerful oligarchy, generally held the field until about the middle of the nineteenth century.[150] But from the 1840's onward the Whig interpretation gained momentum. Macaulay in his second essay on Chatham (1844), based in large part on Walpole's then unpublished *Memoirs of George III*, accepted the legend about George III's subversive education. [151] Lord John Russell in his introduction to the *Bedford Correspondence* (1842-6) took from Burke's *Present Discontents* and other sources the belief that George III had tried to overthrow the constitution. But the Whig myth did not achieve full academic orthodoxy until the appearance in 1861 of May's *Constitutional History*. May and Lecky (1882) falsely assumed that under George I and George II ministers with the confidence of Parliament exercised royal power. They assumed also the existence of a system of more or less organized political parties. In true Whig fashion they judged the past in terms of their present[152] and read the nineteenth-century constitution back into the 1760's. They ended by accusing George III of standing in the path of progress by hindering the development of responsible Parliamentary government. Lecky spoke of George III's "determination to restore the royal power to a position wholly different from that which it occupied in the reign of his predecessor," and Trevelyan took much the same view.[153] William Hunt in his article on George III in the *Dictionary of National Biography* (1890) and in volume ten of the *Political History of England* (1905) perpetuated the Whig interpretation. Hunt, it may be added, had considerable prestige among twentieth-century historians. Actually there were no organized political parties of the modern sort in England in the eighteenth century, and the system of cabinet responsibility to Parliament had not yet evolved.[154] George III, like his grandfather, was "the hereditary, irresponsible head of the executive in a Parliamentary state," [155] and, as such, within his constitutional rights when he insisted on selecting his own ministers and freely using the patronage (or influence) at the disposal of the Crown. Nonetheless, despite the heroic efforts on the part of a number of scholars to dispel the myths about George III, in 1937 there appeared this remarkable statement: "George III tried to break the unconstitutional tyranny of the Whigs by establishing unconstitutional autocracy" [156]—a sentence which contains both the Whig and Tory versions of the myth in thoroughly garbled form.

It is impossible to determine with exactitude the extent of Horace Walpole's contribution to the mythology surrounding George III, but any estimate will allocate to him a large share of the responsibility. Walpole's *Memoirs of George III* appeared (1845) about the same time that a number of other eighteenth-century papers containing materials hostile to George III were published, such as the *Chatham Correspondence* (1838-40), *Bedford Correspondence* (1842-6), *Burke Correspondence* (1844), Harris' *Hardwicke* (1847), Albemarle's *Rockingham* (1852), and the *Grenville Papers* (1852-3). On the other hand Walpole's memoirs had an attraction beyond that of most of these papers, in that the memoirs were written in an especially lively and convincing manner. Editors of eighteenth-century papers published after 1822 regularly used Walpole in their annotations as corroboratory evidence. Walpole's interpretation of the reign of George III was particularly influential on the writings of Macaulay, May, Lecky, and Hunt. [157]

It has been said that in using Walpole's memoirs "a safe working rule to proceed on is that his facts are first-class and his generalizations worthless." [158] The contrary can be maintained, for many of Walpole's "facts" are incorrect, while his generalizations remain of inestimable value, not in the sense of their being true, but in that they constitute a most useful expression of the intellectual climate of his period. Even the "Journal 1783-91," which is of scant value as a factual source, is vibrant with Whiggish indignation at George III and the younger Pitt. Indeed, Walpole's memoirs have had their greatest influence not because of their facts but because of the attitudes which they embody. [159] In many ways Walpole was an ideal mirror to reflect the political hopes and fears of his class, for he was active, inquisitive, and impressionable, as well as unusually articulate. For purposes of understanding the impact which politics made upon his generation, Walpole's memoirs are unexcelled, because they present in miniature the apprehensions, prejudices, fictions, ethical standards, and political ideals of the Whig section of the English aristocracy in the eighteenth century.

NOTES

··

Chapter 1.

1. Gray to Walpole, December [15, 1746], *The Yale Edition of Horace Walpole's Correspondence*, ed. Wilmarth S. Lewis and others (New Haven, 1937-), *14*, 9; the manuscript of the "Memoires" is in the possession of W. S. Lewis.

2. Walpole's "Short Notes" of his life, *Correspondence* (Yale edn.), *13*, 23, 42.

3. In the possession of W. S. Lewis.

4. Walpole's memorandum is in his *Memoirs of George II, I,* pp. v-vi, and in his *Memoirs of George III, I,* pp. xvi-xvii.

5. Walpole to George, fifth Earl Waldegrave, not dated (unpublished, in the possession of W. S. Lewis).

6. Lord Holland's edition (2 vols., London) was republished (3 vols., London) in 1847.

7. *Memoirs of George II, 1,* p. vii.

8. Le Marchant's edition (4 vols., London) was succeeded in 1894 by that of G. F. Russell Barker (also 4 vols., London). Certain passages in the memoirs, deleted by the editors, are in Romney Sedgwick, "Horace Walpole," in *From Anne to Victoria,* ed. Bonamy Dobrée (London, 1937), pp. 271-3, 276-7.

9. Dr. Doran's edition (2 vols., London) was republished in 1910 (2 vols., London) edited by Archibald F. Steuart.

10. Walpole to Montagu, October 11, 1759. Unless otherwise stated all references to Walpole's letters are to the Yale edition in progress, which supersedes that of Mrs. Paget Toynbee (16 vols., Oxford, 1903-5, with supplement, 3 vols., 1918-25).

11. Louis Kronenberger, *Kings and Desperate Men* (New York, 1942), p. 315.

12. Williams to Selwyn, October 19, 1764, quoted in Robert W. Ketton-Cremer, *Horace Walpole* (New York, 1940), p. 18.

13. Walpole to Montagu, October 24, 1758.

14. Walpole to Mann, March 7, 1754.

15. Boswell's *Johnson*, ed. G. B. Hill, rev. by L. F. Powell (Oxford, 1934-40), *2*, 365-6; Chesterfield to Mrs. Howard, July 26, 1729, Chesterfield's *Letters*, ed. Bonamy Dobrée (London, 1932), *2*, 119-20; Voltaire's *Philosophical Dictionary*, article on history.

16. John Pinkerton, *Walpoliana* (2 vols., London, [1799]), *1*, 60.

17. Walpole's *Works*, ed. Mary Berry (5 vols., London, 1798), *2*, 105, 107.

18. "Detached Thoughts," *ibid.*, *4*, 368; see also *A Note Book of Horace Walpole*, ed. W. S. Lewis (New York, 1927), p. 49.

19. Walpole to Lady Ossory, November 4, 1786.

20. Walpole to Lord Hailes, January 23, 1770.

21. *Memoirs of George III, 2*, 114.

22. Wilmarth S. Lewis, *Horace Walpole's Library* (Cambridge, 1958); *Catalogue of the Classic Contents of Strawberry Hill Collected by Horace Walpole, 25 April—21 May, 1842;* Macaulay's *Works* (London, 1914), *8*, 314-15.

23. Walpole to Cole, May 21, 1778; see also, to Mason, March 13, 1777.

24. Walpole's *Notes on the Poems of Alexander Pope*, contributed by Sir W. A. Fraser (London, 1871); Walpole's "Marginal Notes, Written in Dr. Mathy's Miscellaneous Works and Memoirs of the Earl of Chesterfield," ed. R. S. Turner, Philobiblon Society *Miscellanies* (1867-8); *Satirical Poems . . . by William Mason, with Notes by Horace Walpole*, ed. Paget Toynbee (Oxford, 1926); *The Works of . . . Sir Charles Hanbury Williams . . . with Notes by Horace Walpole* (3 vols., London, 1822).

25. See, for example, *Catalogue of Strawberry Hill*, third day, item 202; sixth day, item 20, 65; seventh day, item 42.

26. *A Note Book of Horace Walpole, passim.* His jottings on the back of Cole's letters are printed in the *Walpole-Cole Correspondence* (Yale edn.). He wrote a character sketch of George III on the back of a letter from Mrs. Dickenson dated

September 22, 1788 (unpublished, in the possession of W. S. Lewis). See also *Letters of Horace Walpole*, ed. John Wright (London, 1840), *6*, p. xx.

27. Walpole's *Reminiscences*, ed. Paget Toynbee (Oxford, 1924), pp. 101-46.

28. *Walpole-Du Deffand Correspondence* (Yale edn.), *5*, 367-9.

29. *Last Journals*, *2*, 256, 468; also two sheets of notes in the "Journal 1783-91".

30. *Memoirs of George III*, *2*, 218; Walpole to Hertford, February 15, 1764; Walpole to Bedford, January 22, 1752 (unpublished, transcript in the possession of W. S. Lewis).

31. *Last Journals*, *2*, 442; also *1*, 532, and *2*, 411-12.

32. See Allen T. Hazen, *A Bibliography of Horace Walpole* (New Haven, 1948).

33. Walpole to Montague, June 23, 1750.

34. Carl L. Becker, "Horace Walpole's Memoirs of the Reign of George the Third," *American Historical Review* (1911), *16*, 261.

35. Swift's *Journal to Stella*, March 14, 1713, ed. J. K. Moorhead [John Kirkby] (Everyman edn., 1940), p. 422.

36. Gray to Walpole, December [15, 1746] and October 8, 1751, *Correspondence* (Yale edn.), *14*, 9, 53; Walpole to Montagu, June 6, 1752 and December 23, 1759; Ketton-Cremer, *Horace Walpole*, p. 127; cf. *Letters from George III to Lord Bute*, ed. Romney Sedgwick (London, 1939), p. xl.

37. Pinkerton, *Walpoliana*, *1*, p. xi.

38. John C. Major, *The Role of Personal Memoirs in English Biography and Novel* (Philadelphia, 1935), pp. 9-10, 41, 51.

39. Gilbert Burnet, *Memoires of . . . Hamilton and Castleherald* (London, 1677), preface, p. [ii]; Edouard Fueter, *Histoire de l'historiographie moderne*, trans. Emile Jenmarie (Paris, 1914), pp. 216, 220; Oliver Elton, *A Summary of English Literature 1730-1780* (London, 1928), *2*, 270; L. Rice-Oxley, *Memoirs as a Source of English History* (Oxford, 1914), pp. 10-16.

40. Major, *Role of Personal Memoirs*, pp. 94-6.

41. "Commonplace Book," pp. 9-10 (unpublished, in the possession of W. S. Lewis).

42. "Memoires, from the Declaration of the War with Spain," pp. 2-3.

43. Ketton-Cremer, *Horace Walpole*, p. 193; John Mason, *Gentlefolk in the Making* (Philadelphia, 1935), pp. 193-4, 197.

44. Walpole to Mason, May 15, 1773.

45. Walpole to Lady Ossory, December 12, 1786.

46. Walpole to Robertson, March 4, 1759; Ketton-Cremer, *Horace Walpole*, pp. 278-81.

47. Walpole to Cole, September 22, 1777; Burnet, *Memoires*, preface, p. [ii].

48. Quoted in Rice-Oxley, *Memoirs as a Source of English History*, p. 15.

49. Walpole to Robertson, [1759] (Toynbee edn., *4*, 231).

50. *Memoirs of George II, 1*, pp. xxxii-xxxv; *Memoirs of George III, 1*, 3; *Last Journals, 1*, 265, 514.

51. *Memoirs of George II, 3*, 249; see also *3*, 35, and *Memoirs of George III, 3*, 208.

52. *Memoirs of George II, 1*, 374, and *2*, 48; *Memoirs of George III, 1*, 83, and *3*, 214.

53. Carl L. Becker, *The Heavenly City of the Eighteenth-Century Philosophers* (New Haven, 1932), p. 142.

54. James W. Thompson, *A History of Historical Writing* (New York, 1942), *1*, 88; Major, *Role of Personal Memoirs*, p. 17; Clarendon, *History of the Rebellion*, ed. W. D. Macray (Oxford, 1888), *1*, 1; Cardinal de Retz, *Memoirs* (London, 1896), p. 169; Lord Hervey, *Memoirs*, ed. Romney Sedgwick (London, 1931), *1*, 80; J. B. Black, *The Art of History* (London, 1926), p. 159.

55. Thomas T. Peardon, *The Transition in English Historical Writing 1760-1830* (New York, 1933), pp. 22, 29-30, 34, 193; Thompson, *History of Historical Writing, 2*, 73, 89.

56. A clear statement of this point is in Dorothy A. Koch, "English Theories concerning the Nature and Uses of History 1735-1791" (Yale doctoral dissertation, 1946), pp. xxxi, 115.

57. *Memoirs of George II, 1*, 374, see also *1*, 372, and *2*, 30; *Memoirs of George III, 1*, 2, and *2*, 114; *Last Journals, 1*, 73, and *2*, 440.

58. *Memoirs of George III, 2*, 7.

59. *Ibid.*, 2, 202.

60. Gilbert Burnet, *History of My Own Time*, ed. Osmund Airy (Oxford, 1897), *1*, p. xxxii; see also *1*, 53.

61. *Memoirs*, ed. Sedgwick, *1*, 2.

62. *Memoirs of George II*, 2, 30; *Memoirs of George III*, *1*, 218, and *2*, 308; *Last Journals*, *1*, 73, 230; Walpole to Mann, August 3, 1775, May 16, 1781, and January 8, 1784; to Lady Ossory, February 1, 1775, and December 15, 1786.

63. *Memoirs of George III*, *1*, 3; see also *Memoirs of George II*, *3*, 164-5, 287-8n.

64. *Memoirs of George III*, 2, 7.

65. Charlotte Lennox, *Memoirs . . . of Madame de Maintenon* (London, 1757), *1*, p. xi.

66. Black, *Art of History*, p. 131; Thompson, *History of Historical Writing*, 2, 73.

67. *Memoirs of George III*, 4, 85.

68. *Ibid.*, 2, 114.

69. *Ibid.*, *1*, 2.

70. Walpole to Lady Ossory, October 23, 1784.

71. Walpole to Lord Beauchamp, March 13, 1762 (unpublished, in the possession of W. S. Lewis).

72. Walpole to Montagu, December 16, 1764.

73. Koch, "English Theories concerning . . . History," p. 1; Chesterfield to his son, November 20, 1739, Chesterfield's *Letters*, ed. Dobrée, *2*, 396-7. Becker believed that Walpole changed his purpose and became didactic in later years (*American Historical Review* [1911,] *16*, 503-4).

74. *Memoirs of George III*, 2, 274.

75. *Ibid.*, *3*, 124-5; see also *4*, 85.

Chapter 2.

1. Peardon, *Transition in English Historical Writing*, pp. 22, 29, 34, 193, 197; Fueter, *Histoire de l'historiographie*, p. 453.

2. *Memoirs of George III*, 2, 114.

3. Major, *Role of Personal Memoirs*, p. 96.

4. *Memoirs of George II, 1,* 7, 70, 102–3, 148.

5. Walpole to West, January 24, 1740.

6. Herbert Butterfield, *The Statecraft of Machiavelli* (London, 1940), p. 30.

7. Black, *Art of History,* pp. 56, 96.

8. Koch, "English Theories concerning . . . History," p. 319.

9. Black, *Art of History,* pp. 56, 97.

10. José Ortega y Gasset, *Concord and Liberty,* trans. Helene Weyl (New York, 1946), p. 148; see also his *Towards a Philosophy of History* (New York, 1941), pp. 217-21.

11. *Memoirs of George II, 1,* 373; *Memoirs of George III, 2,* 114, and *3,* 124; see also Walpole to Pinkerton, October 27, 1784.

12. *Works, 2,* 108.

13. Cicero's *Philippics* (V, x, 1-2); De Retz, *Memoirs,* p. 43; Swift's *Works,* ed. Sir Walter Scott (Edinburgh, 1824), *4,* 326; Chesterfield to Mrs. Howard, July 26, 1729, Chesterfield's *Letters,* ed. Dobrée, *2,* 120; Hervey's *Memoirs,* ed. Sedgwick, *1,* 9, 46, 273.

14. Black, *Art of History,* p. 95; Lennox, *Memoirs of . . . Madame de Maintenon, 1,* p. vi; Nathaniel Wraxall, *Historical and Posthumous Memoirs,* ed. H. B. Wheatley (5 vols., London, 1884), *1,* 3.

15. *Oxford Dictionary of English Proverbs* (Oxford, 1935); Black, *Art of History,* p. 40.

16. Major, *Role of Personal Memoirs,* p. 73.

17. Frederick J. Teggart, *Theory of History* (New Haven, 1925), p. 61.

18. Benedetto Croce, *History,* trans. Douglas Ainslie (New York, 1921), p. 101; *Theory and Practice in Historical Study* (Social Science Research Council Bulletin No. 54, New York, 1946), p. 136, n. 3.

19. Walpole to Montagu, July 16, 1764.

20. Ketton-Cremer, *Horace Walpole,* p. 203; Walpole to Montagu, May 5, 1781.

21. Walpole to Montagu, July 22, 1751, and August 20, 1758.

22. Paris Journals, Anecdotes, 1766, *Walpole-Du Deffand Correspondence* (Yale edn.), *5*, 358-9; Ketton-Cremer, *Horace Walpole*, pp. 280-1; *Catalogue of Strawberry Hill*, sixth day, items 82-160.

23. Basil Williams, *The Whig Supremacy* (Oxford, 1939), p. 368.

24. Thompson, *History of Historical Writing, 2*, 37-45; H. B. Walters, *The English Antiquaries* (London, 1934); Burnet, *Memoires*, preface, p. [ii].

25. *Memoirs of George II, 1*, p. xxxii.

26. *Ibid., 3*, 158-9.

27. *Memoirs of George III, 3*, 107, 124.

28. *Ibid., 2*, 152, 223.

29. *Ibid., 1*, 212 and *4*, 93n; Walpole to Montagu, April 22, 1763; to Lady Ossory, August 19, 1784; *Works, 1*, 532; *Memoirs of George II, 1*, 437-41. Waldegrave's memoirs were first published in 1821.

30. *Memorials and Correspondence of Charles James Fox*, ed. Lord John Russell (4 vols., London, 1853-7), *2*, 57.

31. *Memoirs of George II, 1*, p. xxxii, also 76n, 191n, 223n, and *3*, 214; *Memoirs of George III, 2*, 152, *3*, 168, and *4*, 148, 161; *Last Journals, 1*, 521, and *2*, 238.

32. *Works, 1*, 421.

33. Burnet, *History of My Own Time, 1*, p. xxxiii.

34. *Memoirs of the Duke de Saint-Simon*, trans. Francis Arkwright (London, 1918), *6*, 526-7, 529; Walpole to Lady Ossory, October 19, 1788.

35. Clarendon, *History of the Rebellion, 1*, 3; Edmund Ludlow, *Memoirs*, ed. C. H. Firth (Oxford, 1894), *1*, 9; Richard Bulstrode, *Memoirs* (London, 1721), p. 3, Lennox, *Memoirs . . . of Madame de Maintenon, 1*, 145; Hervey's *Memoirs*, ed. Sedgwick, *2*, 347; Wraxall's *Memoirs, 1*, 3.

36. *Last Journals, 1*, 265.

37. *Memoirs of George II, 3*, 161-2.

38. Burnet, *History of My Own Time, 1*, p. xxxiv; Koch, "English Theories concerning . . . History," p. 53.

39. *Memoirs of George II, 1*, 374.

40. *Ibid., 1*, 238.

41. *Ibid., 1,* 374-5.

42. *Ibid., 1,* 237.

43. *Works, 1,* 387, also *1,* 501.

44. Walpole to Dalrymple, July 11, [1758].

45. *Memoirs of George II, 1,* 375.

46. *Memoirs of George III, 1,* 3.

47. *Memoirs of George II, 1,* 238; see also Walpole to Lord Hailes, November 5, 1766.

48. *Memoirs of George II, 1,* pp. xxxiii-xxxv, 374; *Memoirs of George III, 1,* 84.

49. *Memoirs of George II, 3,* 176.

50. "Memoires, from the Declaration of the War with Spain," p. 3; see also *Last Journals, 1,* 514.

51. *Memoirs of George III, 4,* 85.

52. Koch, "English Theories concerning . . . History," p. 23; Waldo H. Dunn, *English Biography* (London, 1916), p. 93; Burnet, *Memoires,* preface, p. [i]; Lennox, *Memoirs . . . of Madame de Maintenon, 1,* p. vii; Clarendon, *History of the Rebellion, 1,* 3; Hervey's *Memoirs,* ed. Sedgwick, *1,* 1-2.

53. Quoted in Black, *Art of History,* p. 91.

54. Koch, "English Theories concerning . . . History," pp. 139, 145-7; Count Grammont, *Memoirs,* ed. Allan Fea (London, 1906), p. 26; De Retz, *Memoirs,* p. 1; Wraxall's *Memoirs, 1,* 2.

55. Teggart, *Theory of History,* p. 31; Saint-Simon, *Memoirs, 6,* 527.

56. Walpole himself used this term. See Walpole to Mann, April 13, 1762, and September 19, 1781; to Mason, March 2, 1773; and to Beloe, undated (Toynbee edn., *15,* 335).

57. *Memoirs of George III, 1,* 162, and *2,* 114.

58. Burnet, *Memoires,* preface, p. [i]; Black, *Art of History,* p. 13.

59. Walpole to Mann, May 7, 1775; to Pinkerton, October 27, 1784; to Mason, May 7, 1775; to John Nichols, October 31, 1781; to Hannah More, July 12, 1788.

60. *Memoirs of George II, 1,* 372, 374, and *2,* 48.

Chapter 3.

1. Macaulay's *Works*, *8*, 327.
2. *Constitutional History of England* (London, 1867), *2*, 290.
3. *History of England* (Boston, 1853), *2*, 209n.
4. *History of the United States* (Boston, 1854), *5*, 259, n. 4.
5. *History of England in the Eighteenth Century* (London, 1892), *2*, 125n, 172-3; *Life of Edward Lord Hawke* (London, 1896), pp. 46, 59, 236.
6. *Quarterly Review* (1822), *27*, 178; (1843), *72*, 516; (1844), *74*, 395; (1846), *77*, 253; (1848), *83*, 110; (1851), *89*, 135. A summary of Croker's views is given in Herbert Butterfield, *George III and the Historians* (London, 1957), pp. 122-31.
7. *Memorials and Correspondence of C. J. Fox*, *1*, 273.
8. The Queen to Lady Harcourt, July 11, 1798, *The Harcourt Papers* (privately printed, Oxford, 1876-1903), *6*, 59.
9. Sir Lewis Namier, *Monarchy and the Party System* (Oxford, 1952), pp. 5, 25.
10. Butterfield, *George III and the Historians*, pp. 261-70; Richard Pares, *King George III and the Politicians* (Oxford, 1953), pp. 47n, 72, 90n, 92n.
11. Herbert Butterfield, *George III, Lord North, and the People 1779-80* (London, 1949), p. 388.
12. Sedgwick in *From Anne to Victoria*, ed. Dobrée, p. 266.
13. *Horace Walpole's Fugitive Verse*, ed. W. S. Lewis (New York, 1931); Walpole to Mason, May 11, 1769; to Nichols, October 31, 1781; and to Pinkerton, October 27, 1784.
14. *Memoirs of George III*, *1*, 3, 184, 307, and *2*, 7, 114, 274. The italics in this paragraph are my own.
15. Black, *Art of History*, p. 32; also authorities cited above in note 73, chapter 1.
16. *Memoirs of George II*, *3*, 164-5.
17. Walpole to Mason, March 3, 1781.
18. *Works*, *2*, 107; *Memoirs of George II*, *1*, 374; Walpole to Mary Berry, July 10, 1790; to Pinkerton, June 26, 1785.

19. Walpole to Strafford, July 4, 1757; to Mason, August 4, 1777, and April 7, 1780; to Lady Ossory, August 19, 1784, and July 17, 1792.

20. Walpole to Mason, February 18, 1776; see also Walpole to Lady Ossory, November 8, 1789.

21. Walpole to Bentley, March 27, 1755; to Zouch, October 21, 1758; to Dalrymple, July 11, [1758].

22. Black, *Art of History*, p. 15.

23. *Memoirs of George III*, 2, 308; see also Pinkerton, *Walpoliana*, 2, 17.

24. *Quarterly Review* (1822), 27, 185.

25. *Memoirs of George III*, 1, 260.

26. *Ibid.*, 1, 176–7.

27. *Works*, 2, 363–70.

28. Walpole's *Reminiscences*, pp. 10–11; Walpole to Mann, February 25, 1782.

29. See George O. Trevelyan, *The Early History of Charles James Fox* (New York, 1881), pp. 61–3; David Cecil, *The Young Melbourne* (London, 1939), pp. 9–15.

30. Walpole to Thomas Walpole, December 9, 1787.

31. Walpole to Mann, December 13, 1759; to Mary Berry, October 31, 1790, and August 16, 1796; see also Ketton-Cremer, *Horace Walpole*, p. 42.

32. Walpole to Lady Ossory, June 28, 1782; to Mann, July 24, 1749; to Mason, May 15, 1773; to the Earl of Buchan, September 23, 1785; to Lord Hertford, February 6, 1764; to Thomas Walpole, December 9, 1787.

33. Walpole to Hannah More, November 4, 1789.

34. Walpole's "Short Notes" of his life (*Correspondence*, Yale edn., *13*, 5); Walpole's "Book of Materials, 1759," p. 16 (in the Folger Library, photostat in the possession of W. S. Lewis) has a section entitled "Nonsense of the Law." See also Walpole to Mann, February 3, 1760, and June 20, 1762.

35. Walpole to Robert Jephson, [February, 1775].

36. Walpole to Lady Ossory, June 28, 1782.

37. Walpole to Lady Ossory, August 9, 1773; to Mason, October 5, 1777.

38. Walpole to Lady Ossory, January 19, 1777.

39. Walpole to Robert Jephson, [February, 1775].

40. Macaulay's *Works*, 8, 326; Sedgwick in *From Anne to Victoria*, ed. Dobrée, p. 277; Leslie Stephen, *Hours in a Library* (2nd. ser., London, 1876), p. 168; Austen Dobson, *Horace Walpole* (London, 1927), p. 289; Gamaliel Bradford, *Bare Souls* (London, 1924), p. 100; George Saintsbury, *The Peace of the Augustans* (London, 1916), pp. 225, 228.

41. *Memoirs of George II, 1*, 205.

42. *Works, 1*, 456.

43. *Memoirs of George II, 1*, 230–6.

44. *Ibid., 1*, 94.

45. *Ibid., 3*, 39.

46. *Ibid., 3*, 39n; Macaulay's *Works*, 8, 327. Further discussion of Walpole's use of antithesis is in Paul Yvon, *Horace Walpole* (Paris, 1924), p. 218, and in *Memorials and Correspondence of C. J. Fox, 2*, 8.

47. Walpole to Robertson, [1759] (Toynbee edn., *4*, 231).

48. *Memoirs of George II, 1*, 89, 147–50, and *2*, 264; *Memoirs of George III, 1*, 192, 307, and *2*, 312–13; *Last Journals, 2*, 229.

49. *Memoirs of George III, 1*, 31.

50. Sir Lewis Namier, *The Structure of Politics at the Accession of George III* (London, 1929), pp. 202, 258–9. A few payments had been made in advance during the lifetime of George II. See also pp. 195–6 for Walpole's incorrect statements about this election in his letter to Mann, March 3, 1761.

51. See Butterfield, *George III and the Historians*, p. 109.

52. Lord Spencer's letters to his mother, December 21 and 22, 1783, and Pitt to Lord Spencer, December 21, 1783, in Keith G. Feiling, *The Second Tory Party 1714–1832* (London, 1938), pp. 397–8; extracts from Lord Temple's exchange of letters with George III on December 21, 1783, in Donald G. Barnes, *George III and William Pitt 1783–1806* (Stanford, 1939), pp. 71–2; Fox's letter of December 30, 1783, in *Memorials and Correspondence of C. J. Fox, 2*, 223; Elliot to Harris, January 1, 1784, in *Diaries and Correspondence of James Harris, first Earl of Malmesbury*, ed. James, third Earl of Malmesbury (4 vols., London, 1844), *2*, 59.

53. *Memoirs of George III, 1*, 283; see also Walpole to Mann, February 25, 1742.

54. Walpole to Cole, May 4, 1774; to Lady Ossory, June 20, 1781; to Mann, August 26, 1785.

55. Pinkerton, *Walpoliana, 1*, 88; see also William Coxe, *Memoirs of . . . Sir Robert Walpole* (London, 1800), *3*, 349–50, and Walpole's "Book of Materials, 1759," p. 44.

Chapter 4.

1. Lecky, *History of England in the Eighteenth Century, 2*, 172; Feiling, *Second Tory Party*, p. 66.

2. "Detached Thoughts," in *Works, 4*, 369; Walpole to Mann, December 31, 1769, and March 5, 1772; to Lady Ossory, August 16, 1776, January 19, 1777, and August 26, 1784. This was a favorite saying of Melbourne (Cecil, *The Young Melbourne*, p. 263).

3. *Memoirs of George II, 3*, 162.

4. Walpole to Lady Ossory, December 9, 1790, and June 14, 1787; see also Walpole to Mason, October 4, 1773.

5. Walpole to Chute, August 20, 1743; to Lord Harcourt, October 18, 1777.

6. *Memoirs of George II, 2*, 255.

7. *Walpole-Cole Correspondence* (Yale edn.), *2*, 372; Selwyn to Carlisle, [October, 1775], Historical Manuscripts Commission, *15th Report, Appendix VI* (1897), p. 298.

8. *Memoirs of George II, 2*, 327–8.

9. *Memoirs of George III, 1*, 320. General warrants, which did not specify the names of the persons accused, had been used in the arrest of John Wilkes in 1763. Their doubtful legality evoked much protest. See Lecky, *History of England in the Eighteenth Century, 3*, 246–58.

10. Ketton-Cremer, *Horace Walpole*, pp. 211–19.

11. *Hours in a Library*, 2nd ser., p. 166.

12. Ketton-Cremer, *Horace Walpole*, pp. 78–84, 147–9, 228, 240, 247, 286–7, 324.

13. Paul E. More, *Shelbourne Essays* (4th ser., London, 1906), p. 261.

14. *Memoirs of George III, 1*, 84, *2*, 209, and *3*, 25.

15. Lord Ossory's memorandum, May, 1814 (unpublished, in the possession of W. S. Lewis).

16. *Memorials and Correspondence of C. J. Fox, 1*, 273; *Letters of Horace Walpole . . . to Horace Mann* (New York, 1833), *1*, p. xxxi; Ketton-Cremer, *Horace Walpole*, p. 140.

17. *Memoirs of George III, 4*, 130.

18. *Ibid., 1*, 143.

19. *Last Journals, 1*, 513.

20. *Memoirs of George III, 4*, 196–7.

21. In *Memoirs of George II* (*1*, 46) this passage was deleted by the editor. It is supplied from photostats of the manuscript which are in the possession of W. S. Lewis.

22. Another deleted passage (*Memoirs of George III, 2*, 32), also supplied from photostats in the possession of W. S. Lewis.

23. *Last Journals, 2*, 466.

24. *Memoirs of George II, 1*, 141. The last sentence was deleted by the editor and is given (with other suppressed passages) in Sedgwick's article in *From Anne to Victoria*, ed. Dobrée, p. 272.

25. *Memoirs of George III, 1*, 219.

26. *Walpole-Mann Letters* (1833), pp. xxx–xxxi.

27. Hervey's *Memoirs*, ed. Sedgwick, *1*, 162, and *3*, 671, 677, 681.

28. J. K. Moorhead [John Kirkby] in the preface to Swift's *Journal to Stella* (Everyman edn.) p. xxi.

29. William P. Sandford, *English Theories of Public Address* (Ohio State University, 1929), pp. 90–1, 132–3, 198–200.

30. Chesterfield to his son, July 9, 1750, Chesterfield's *Letters*, ed. Dobrée, *4*, 1562.

31. Chesterfield to his son, December 5, 1749, and February 11, 1751, *ibid., 4*, 1454, 1678–9.

32. Wraxall's *Memoirs, 2*, 119.

33. Ketton-Cremer, *Horace Walpole*, p. 20.

34. *Memoirs of George II, 2*, 143–9; *Last Journals, 1*, 80; Walpole to Mann, April 9, 1772.

35. *Memoirs of George II*, 2, 62, 154; *Last Journals*, 2, 76; *The Diaries of Sylvester Douglas (Lord Glenbervie)*, ed. Francis Bickley (London, 1928), *1*, 251–2.

36. Philip Magnus, *Edmund Burke* (London, 1939), pp. 213-20, 239-40.

37. See, for example, *Memoirs of George II*, 3, 8; *Memoirs of George III*, *1*, 176-7.

38. Walpole to Mann, May 12, 1767; *Memoirs of George III*, 3, 17; *Glenbervie Diaries*, *1*, 52; Wraxall's *Memoirs*, *1*, 260, and 3, 221, 362.

39. *Memoirs of George II*, 3, 165; *Memoirs of George III*, *1*, 2; Walpole to Mason, March 3, 1781; to Selwyn, December 2, 1765. The italics in this passage are my own.

40. Sir James Harris to his son, November 23, 1778, in Earl of Malmesbury, *Letters* (London, 1870), *1*, 396.

41. *Glenbervie Diaries*, *1*, 326; Wraxall's *Memoirs*, 4, 139, 266, and 5, 264.

42. *The Parliamentary History of England*, ed. William Cobbett and John Wright (36 vols., London, 1806–20), *22*, 47; George III to Pitt, March 6, 1788, in Earl Stanhope, *Life of . . . Pitt* (4 vols., London, 1861–2), *1*, p. xxiii.

43. Walpole to Mann, July 6, 1775; see also to Hertford, November 25, 1764, and to Mann, July 12, 1765.

44. *Memoirs of George II*, 3, 85. The others were the elder Pitt, the Duke of Cumberland, Lord Mansfield, and Lord Granville.

45. Walpole to Mann, August 19, 1779.

46. Walpole to Pownall, October 27, 1783; to Zouch, October 21, 1758; to Lord Hailes, January 1, 1781.

47. *Memoirs of George II*, *1*, 226, 234; Walpole to Montagu, May 16, 1759.

48. George Hardinge in John Nichols, *Literary Anecdotes of the Eighteenth Century* (9 vols., London, 1812-15), 8, 526.

49. *Memoirs of George II*, *1*, 32, 70.

50. *Memoirs of George III*, 3, 260–1.

51. *Memoirs of George II*, *1*, 53–4; see also *Memoirs of George III*, *1*, 58.

52. *Memoirs of George II, 1,* 52; see also Walpole to Mann, December 10, 1741, and February 9, 1742.

53. See above, p. 37.

54. *Memoirs of George II, 1,* 110.

55. *Ibid., 1,* 118.

56. See above, p. 38.

57. Walpole's "Short Notes" of his life (*Correspondence,* Yale edn., *13,* 19).

58. *Memoirs of George II, 1,* 3, 168–70, and *3,* 85.

59. *Ibid., 1,* 167, 168n.

60. *Ibid., 1,* 162, 166.

61. Walpole to Mann, February 1, 1745; see also *Memoirs of George III, 2,* 149.

62. *Memoirs of George II, 1,* 373.

63. *Ibid., 1,* 164.

64. *Ibid., 1,* 159–61. The words "man . . . principles" in the first sentence were deleted by the editor and are printed in Philip C. Yorke, *Life . . . of . . . Hardwicke* (3 vols., Cambridge, 1913), *1,* 569n.

65. *Ibid.*

66. *Ibid., 1,* 278; *Memoirs of George II, 1,* 159, 165; Ketton-Cremer, *Horace Walpole,* p. 140.

67. *Memoirs of George II, 1,* 92–3, *2,* 55, 99, and *3,* 85, 175, 287n; *Memoirs of George III, 1,* 53, and *2,* 119, 274.

68. *Memoirs of George II, 2,* 149, and *3,* 173, 176; *Memoirs of George III, 2,* 259; Walpole to Mann, June 11, 1758.   ,

69. *Memoirs of George II, 3,* 160.

70. *Memoirs of George III, 2,* 273; also *1,* 173, *2,* 223, 270, 280, and *4,* 105.

71. *Ibid., 1,* 321; *Memoirs of George II, 1,* 7, 93, and *3,* 156; Walpole to Conway, October 17, 1758; to Mann, February 23, 1747.

72. Walpole to Langley, March 13, 1767; Walpole's "Short Notes" of his life (*Correspondence,* Yale edn., *13,* 38); *Works, 2,* 369; Walpole to Mann, September 1, 1747, June 9, 1757, August 18, 1767, and May 5, 1782; to Lady Ossory, November 1, 1779; *Memoirs of George II, 2,* 169; *Memoirs of George III, 2,* 149.

73. Ketton-Cremer, *Horace Walpole,* p. 111; *Works, 2,* 365;

Walpole to Harcourt, [1780] (Toynbee edn., *11*, 236–9). *Wal-pole* held three sinecures for life: Usher of the Exchequer, Comptroller of the Pipe, and Clerk of the Escheat. He had a share in the office of Collector of the Customs, which lapsed at the death of his brother Edward in 1784 (*Works*, *2*, 363–70). He held a fifth sinecure, the office of Inspector General of Exports and Imports in the Custom House, only from December 7, 1737, to February 13, 1737/8 (Cokayne's *Peerage* under Orford).

74. *Works*, *2*, 371–91.

75. *Ibid.*, *2*, 367; Walpole to Conway, October 31, 1776; *Memoirs of George III*, *1*, 167, 210 and *3*, 68n; *Last Journals*, *1*, 488; Walpole's "Short Notes" of his life (*Correspondence*, Yale edn., *13*, 38).

76. *Works*, *2*, 366–7.

77. *Letters from George III to Lord Bute*, ed. Sedgwick, pp. xxxix-xlii; see also Sedgwick's article in *From Anne to Victoria*, ed. Dobrée, p. 275, where mention is made of Walpole's "repeated application" to Pelham.

78. *Memoirs of George III*, *2*, 4–5.

79. Ketton-Cremer, *Horace Walpole*, pp. 23–4, 52; the other two were his love for his mother and for Mary Berry.

80. Walpole to Conway, July 4, 1761.

81. *Memoirs of George III*, *2*, 98.

82. *Ibid.*, *1*, 320, and *2*, 3–5; Ketton-Cremer, *Horace Walpole*, p. 247. The pamphlet, *A Counter Address* etc. (1764) is in *Works*, *2*, 547–76.

83. *Memoirs of George II*, *1*, 384, 414 and *2*, 42; *Memoirs of George III*, *1*, 166.

84. *Memoirs of George II*, *2*, 328; *Memoirs of George III*, *1*, 154, 157, 167, 184, 188.

85. *Memoirs of George III*, *1*, 196.

86. *Ibid.*, *4*, 84.

87. *Ibid.*, *1*, 209.

88. *Memoirs of George II*, *1*, 2, 186, and *3*, 20.

89. *Ibid.*, *1*, 233, 263, and *2*, 313–14; Walpole to Conway, September 9, also October 29, 1762; to Mann, December 8, 1756, and July 12, 1765.

90. *Memoirs of George III*, *1*, 77, 157.

91. *Ibid., 1,* 320–1

92. *Ibid., 1,* 269.

93. *Ibid., 1,* 27, 280, 2, 4, 44, and 3, 67; *Memoirs of George II, 1,* 136; Walpole to Lord Hertford, January 22, 1764; to Lady Ossory, September 29, 1777.

94. *Memoirs of George III, 4,* 84, 125.

95. *Ibid., 1,* 215.

96. *Ibid., 1,* 269–74, 320.

97. *Memoirs of George II, 1,* 47.

98. *Ibid., 2,* 205; *Memoirs of George III, 1,* 15.

99. *Memoirs of George III, 2,* 280n, and 3, 147.

100. *Ibid., 1,* 320.

101. *Last Journals, 1,* 513.

102. "Journal 1783–91" (typescript, ed. Judd, Yale Library), pp. 81–2, 84–6, 94.

103. *Memoirs of George III, 2,* 194, and 4, 28.

Chapter 5.

1. This is the opinion of Basil Williams (*Life of William Pitt, Earl of Chatham* [2 vols., London, 1913], *1,* 270n, and 2, 203n, 336, 346n) and Philip Yorke (*Life of Hardwicke, 2,* 65, n. 3).

2. *Memoirs of George II, 1,* p. xxxiii.

3. *Ibid., 1,* 8–9. In these extracts from Walpole's reports of debates some italics have been removed for the sake of clarity.

4. [John Almon], *Anecdotes of . . . Chatham* (London, 1792), *1,* 188.

5. *Memoirs of George III, 1,* 195.

6. Rigby to Bedford, March 10, 1763, in *Correspondence of John, fourth Duke of Bedford,* ed. Lord John Russell (3 vols., London, 1842–6), *3,* 218.

7. *Memoirs of George III, 2,* 187–8.

8. *Correspondence of William Pitt, Earl of Chatham,* ed. W. S. Taylor and J. H. Pringle (4 vols., London, 1838–40), *2,* 372n.

9. *Last Journals, 1,* 92.

10. Burke in *Chatham Correspondence*, 4, 220n.

11. For example, a number of Pitt's speeches (see Williams, *Life of Chatham*, 2, 342–3, 345, 349).

12. *Memoirs of George II*, 2, 54.

13. *Ibid.*, 2, 48.

14. *Memoirs of George III*, 1, 103, 127, 174–5.

15. *Ibid.*, 1, 249–53; *The Correspondence of King George the third from 1760 to December 1783*, ed. Sir John Fortescue (6 vols., London, 1927–8), 1, 53–7.

16. *Memoirs of George III*, 2, 202.

17. For example, eight undated debates in *ibid.*, 1, 31, 190–2, 265–6; misdated debates in *ibid.*, 1, 282, and in *Last Journals*, 1, 9, 39–40, 77, 89, 162.

18. For example, *Memoirs of George II*, 1, 254, 345; *Memoirs of George III*, 1, 190, 286, and 2, 56, 64, 196; *Last Journals*, 1, 89, 234, where the figures differ from those in the *Journals of the House of Commons*.

19. *Memoirs of George III*, 3, 211n, 214n, 217n.

20. *Ibid.*, 1, 184; *Journals of the House of Commons*, 29, 394–5.

21. For example he stated that 35 (instead of 55) resolutions on the Stamp Act were moved (*Memoirs of George III*, 2, 49); he omitted the name of Hans Stanley from his list of the select committee on India (*Last Journals*, 1, 161); his quotations of the formal proceedings of February 16, 1774, are not verbatim (*ibid.*, 1, 292–3). See *Journals of the House of Commons*, 30, 98–101, and 34, 11, 464–5.

22. *Autobiography and Correspondence of Augustus Henry, third Duke of Grafton*, ed. Sir. W. R. Anson (London, 1898), pp. 140–1.

23. Walpole to Lady Ossory, February 6, 1789.

24. *Memoirs of George III*, 1, 158–60.

25. George III to Bute, October 28, 1762, "38 m. pt 10," in *Letters from George III to Lord Bute*, ed. Sedgwick, p. 152, and in Sir Lewis Namier, *England in the Age of the American Revolution* (London, 1930), pp. 431–2.

26. *Letters from George III to Lord Bute*, ed. Sedgwick, pp. 152–3.

27. Allen's note in *Memoirs of George III, 1,* 159n; Fox to Devonshire, November 2, 1762 (paraphrase), and November 9, 1762 (paraphrase and extracts) in Earl of Ilchester, *Henry Fox, First Lord Holland* (2 vols., London, 1920), 2, 207–9. Devonshire left for Chatsworth on October 29 (Fox to Sandwich, October 30, 1762, in Namier, *England,* p. 432), and on November 5, still at Chatsworth, he wrote an angry reply to Fox (*Letters to Henry Fox Lord Holland,* ed. Earl of Ilchester [London, 1915], p. 165).

28. An extract from Cavendish's own account of his resignation is in *Letters from George III to Lord Bute,* ed. Sedgwick, p. 154. Although endorsed "31 Oct. 1762" it does not give the date of his resignation, but Robert Wilmot's letter to Newcastle of October 31, 1762, states, "Lord George Cavendish is just come to town, and . . . proposes to resign this morning" (British Museum, Add. MS. 32944, f. 181, information from A. J. Watson).

29. *Memoirs of George III, 2,* 117–26.

30. *The Grenville Papers,* ed. William J. Smith (4 vols., London, 1852–3), *3,* 165–71: Grenville's diary and notes.

31. *Ibid.*

32. Grenville to the Chancellor, May 23, 1765, and Grenville's diary, *ibid., 3,* 44, 185–6; George III to Egmont, [May 23, 1765], *Correspondence of George III,* ed. Fortescue, *1,* 113.

33. Grenville's diary in *Grenville Papers, 3,* 187; Egmont's notes in *Correspondence of George III,* ed. Fortescue, *1,* 113–14.

34. Minute of the meeting of May 22, also Grenville's diary, in *Grenville Papers, 3,* 41, 183–4; George III's notes in *Correspondence of George III,* ed. Fortescue, *1,* 166, 172.

35. *Memoirs of George III, 2,* 130–47.

36. *Ibid., 2,* 130n; Bedford to Marlborough, June 13, 1765, *Bedford Correspondence, 3,* 286–8; George III to Northington, June 12, 1765, and to Cumberland, same date, *Correspondence of George III,* ed. Fortescue, *1,* 116–19; Newcastle's *Narrative of the Changes in the Ministry 1765–1767,* ed. Mary Bateson (Camden Society, new series, *59,* 1898), p. 21; Grenville's diary in *Grenville Papers, 3,* 194.

37. Grenville to Sandwich, June 21, 1765, in *Grenville*

Papers, 3, 58–9; diary of Sir Gilbert Elliot, *Bedford Correspondence, 3,* 290n; Sir Charles Yorke's notes of his talk with the king in George Harris, *Life of Lord Chancellor Hardwicke* (3 vols., London, 1847), *3,* 447; Selwyn to Holland, [June 13, 1765], *Letters to Lord Holland,* ed. Ilchester, p. 224; also the accounts of Bedford, George III, Grenville, and Newcastle, cited in note 36, above.

38. That the king made some reply is stated by Bedford, Elliot, Grenville, and Yorke in the accounts cited in notes 36 and 37, above.

39. *Memoirs of the Marquis of Rockingham and his Contemporaries,* ed. George Thomas, Earl of Albemarle (2 vols., London, 1852), *1,* 218–20.

40. *Grafton's Autobiography and Correspondence,* p. 54; Grenville's diary in *Grenville Papers, 3,* 211–17; *Correspondence of George III,* ed. Fortescue, *1,* 153–7; two letters of Sandwich to Bedford, July 10, 1765, *Bedford Correspondence, 3,* 306–11; Lord Digby to Lord Holland, July 10, 1765, *Letters to Lord Holland,* ed. Ilchester, p. 227. In his letter to Lady Suffolk of July 9, 1765, Walpole himself noted that the new ministers had not yet taken office.

41. *Memoirs of George II, 3,* 31–2; *Memoirs of George III, 1,* 99; cf. Yorke, *Life of Hardwicke, 2,* 370 n. 1, 372 n. 2, 400–3; *Bedford Correspondence, 2,* 253.

42. *Memoirs of George III, 2,* 261–2, 281–4; cf. *Bedford Correspondence, 3,* 349–53, 358–9; *Correspondence of George III,* ed. Fortescue, *1,* 419; *Sir Henry Cavendish's Debates,* ed. John Wright (2 vols., London, 1841–3), *1,* 591–3.

43. *Memoirs of George III, 3,* 165–7; cf. Grafton's *Autobiography and Correspondence,* pp. 214–15, 221, 223; *Correspondence of George III,* ed. Fortescue, *2,* 47–50, 54; *Chatham Correspondence, 3,* 338, 340–1; Lord Edmond Fitzmaurice, *Life of William Earl of Shelburne* (3 vols., London, 1912), *1,* 385–7.

44. *Last Journals, 2,* 413–26; cf. *Correspondence of George III,* ed. Fortescue, *5,* 374–6, 382–4, 397; *Memoirs of Rockingham,* ed. Albemarle, *2,* 451; *Memorials and Correspondence of C. J. Fox, 1,* 290, 293, 297; Wraxall's *Memoirs, 1,* 261, and *2,* 258–61; Historical MSS. Commission, *Stopford Sackville MSS., 1,* 141.

For further instances of Walpole's inaccuracy see Yorke, *Life of Hardwicke, 1,* 278, 3, 17 n. 4, and 24 n. 1.

45. *Quarterly Review* (1846), 77, 275.

Chapter 6.

1. Pyle to Kerrich, February 22, 1757, quoted in Ketton-Cremer, *Horace Walpole,* pp. 223–4.

2. *Eclectic Review* (1851), new ser., 2, 683.

3. Isaac Disraeli, *Calamities of Authors* (London, 1812), *1,* 125–7; Alexander Chalmers, *Biographical Dictionary* (London, 1817), *31,* 61; Lord Holland in *Memorials and Correspondence of C. J. Fox, 1,* 273; Thackeray, *The Virginians,* ch. 53.

4. Macaulay's *Works, 8,* 314.

5. John Rhode and Carter Dickson, *Fatal Descent* (New York, Popular Library, [1946]), p. 46.

6. Walpole to Mann. March 22, 1779.

7. Walpole to Conway, September 16, 1777; to Lady Ossory, December 26, 1788; see also to Pinkerton, August 19, 1789.

8. Dobson, *Horace Walpole,* p. 289.

9. For example, *Dublin University Magazine* (1859), *53,* 450; *Temple Bar* (1904), *129,* 156.

10. *Hours in a Library,* 2nd ser., p. 168.

11. Ketton-Cremer, *Horace Walpole,* espec. pp. 17–24; see also Norman Pearson, "Some Neglected Aspects of Horace Walpole," *Fortnightly Review* (1909), *92,* 490; Butterfield, *George III and the Historians,* p. 261.

12. Ketton-Cremer, *Horace Walpole,* pp. 225–7.

13. William Holdsworth, *A History of English Law* (London, 1938), *10,* 714.

14. Zera S. Fink, *The Classical Republicans* (Evanston, 1945), pp. 2–5, 10, 21–4, 186, 190; Stanley M. Pargellis, "The Theory of Balanced Government," in *The Constitution Reconsidered,* ed. Conyers Read (New York, 1938), pp. 39–45; William A. Dunning, *A History of Political Theories from Luther to Montesquieu* (new ed., New York, 1943), pp. 358, 379.

15.   Holdsworth, *History of English Law*, *10*, 8; Becker, *Heavenly City*, pp. 30, 61; Alfred Cobban, *Edmund Burke* (London, 1929), p. 27; Arthur O. Lovejoy, *The Great Chain of Being*, (Cambridge, 1936), pp. 7, 9, 184; Basil Willey, *The Eighteenth-Century Background* (London, 1940), pp. 2–5, 46.

16.   Walpole to Lady Ossory, December 7, 1792.

17.   *Parliamentary History*, *21*, 1269.

18.   [William Stevens], *The Revolution Vindicated* (Cambridge, 1777), p. 31.

19.   Cobban, *Burke*, p. 44; Peardon, *Transition in English Historical Writing*, p. 54; Leslie Stephen, *English Thought in the Eighteenth Century* (new ed., New York, 1927), *2*, 172; Philip A. Brown, *The French Revolution in English History* (London, 1918), p. 39.

20.   George H. Guttridge, *English Whiggism and the American Revolution* (Berkeley, 1942), pp. 7, 10.

21.   *Memoirs of George III*, *1*, 255–6.

22.   *American Historical Review* (1911), *16*, 266, 499.

23.   *Memoirs of George III*, *3*, 123; see also *A Note Book of Horace Walpole*, p. 49.

24.   Walpole's "Miscellany, 1786," p. 35 (in the Folger Library, photostat in the possession of W. S. Lewis).

25.   "Memoires, from the Declaration of the War, with Spain," p. 4.

26.   *Memoirs of George II*, *1*, 376–7; Walpole to Mann, April 20, 1757.

27.   Macaulay's *Works*, *8*, 317.

28.   Walpole's *letters*, ed. Wright (1840), *6*, p. xiii.

29.   *Memoirs of George II*, *1*, 376-7; see also *Last Journals*, *2*, 167; Walpole to Lady Ossory, July 7, 1782, and December 7, 1792.

30.   Ketton-Cremer, *Horace Walpole*, p. 193.

31.   Walpole to Lady Ossory, December 9, 1790.

32.   *Ibid.;* see also Walpole to Mary Berry, May 4, 1791.

33.   Guttridge, *English Whiggism*, pp. 32, 43, 120-1.

34.   Walpole to Mann, November 6, 1769.

35.   *Last Journals*, *2*, 286; see also Walpole to Cole, March 30, 1780.

36.   Walpole to Mason, April 7, 1780.

37. Walpole to Mason, July 4, 1778.

38. Walpole's letter of May 27, 1794, addressee unknown.

39. Walpole to Mann, October 28, 1760; see also Becker in *American Historical Review* (1911), *16*, 262-7; Butterfield, *George III and the Historians*, p. 22.

40. Walpole to Mann, November 1, November 14, and December 5, 1760.

41. Walpole to Montagu, May 26, 1765; see also to Hertford, May 20, 1765, and to Mann, May 25, 1765.

42. Walpole to Mann, January 30, 1770.

43. Walpole to Mann, November 26, 1770.

44. Walpole to Mann, September 7, 1775.

45. *Last Journals*, *2*, 113.

46. Walpole's manuscript entitled "George III" (unpublished, in the possession of W. S. Lewis).

47. Walpole's "George III and his Ministers" in *Extracts from the Journals and Correspondence of Miss Berry*, ed. Lady Theresa Lewis (3 vols., London, 1866), *2*, 59-60. The extract quoted here has been collated with photostats of the manuscript, which are in the possession of W. S. Lewis.

48. Walpole's character sketch of George III on the back of a letter from Mrs. Dickenson, dated September 22, 1788 (unpublished, in the possession of W. S. Lewis).

49. Becker in *American Historical Review* (1911), *16*, 257, 259, 272, 496, 500, 503, 505.

50. Butterfield, *George III and the Historians*, pp. 22, 115-17.

51. Becker in *American Historical Review* (1911), *16*, 269-70.

52. Guttridge, *English Whiggism*, pp. 42-4; *Letters from George III to Lord Bute*, ed. Sedgwick, p. xviii.

53. *Memoirs of George III*, *4*, 87-8, 95-7.

54. *Ibid.*, *4*, 91.

55. *Ibid.*, *4*, 91-4.

56. *Ibid.*, *4*, 90, 95.

57. These proceedings are summarized in *Letters from George III to Lord Bute*, ed. Sedgwick pp. xxiv-xxxvii; the memorial is in *Memoirs of George II*, *1*, 298-302.

58. *Memoirs of George III, 4,* 92.

59. *Ibid., 1,* 158.

60. *Ibid., 3,* 67; see also *Last Journals, 2,* 461-2.

61. *Junius* (Edinburgh, 1807), p. 152; John Nicholls, *Recollections* (2nd ed., London, 1822), *1,* 6, 12.

62. Fitzmaurice, *Shelburne, 1,* 53.

63. Grafton's *Autobiography and Correspondence,* p. 13.

64. Portland to Windham, January 11, 1794, in *The Windham Papers,* ed. Earl of Rosebery (2 vols., London, 1913), *1,* 202.

65. Walpole's "George III" (cited in note 46, above).

66. *Memoirs of George III, 1,* 214, 237, and *2,* 205-6.

67. *Ibid., 3,* 49.

68. *Ibid., 4,* 88-9; *Last Journals, 2,* 506.

69. *Memoirs of George III, 4,* 90n; *Last Journals, 1,* 164.

70. *Memoirs of George III, 4,* 90; *Satirical Poems by Mason with Notes by Horace Walpole,* ed. Toynbee, p. 97.

71. *Memoirs of George III, 4,* 75n.

72. *Ibid., 1,* 19, 27, 34, 110, 139-40, 317, and *2,* 63. For Walpole's use of the term "Jacobite" as a stigma see *ibid., 1,* 140n, 258, and *2,* 103, 298.

73. *Parliamentary History, 19,* 917, and *20,* 1029.

74. *Ibid., 21,* 358, 1284, and *23,* 667.

75. *The True State of the Question* (London, 1784), p. 36.

76. *The Source of the Evil* (London, 1784), p. 9; cf. David Hartley, *Letters on the American War* (London, 1778), pp. 42-3.

77. Chesterfield to his son, July 2, 1765, Chesterfield's *Letters,* ed. Dobrée, *6,* 2657.

78. Wraxall's *Memoirs, 1,* 326, 328.

79. Guttridge, *English Whiggism,* p. 104; *Junius,* pp. 200, 216.

80. *Memoirs of George III, 4,* 84; see also *3,* 136, and *4,* 112, 157.

81. *Last Journals, 2,* 432; see also *2,* 113.

82. "Journal 1783-91" (typescript, Yale Library), p. 112.

83. *Parliamentary History, 20,* 1347, and *22,* 146.

84. Guttridge, *English Whiggism,* p. 104.

85.   Blackstone, *Commentaries*, Bk. IV, ch. 33, p. 441; Burke's *Works* (Boston, 1866), *1*, 444; see also [John Douglas], *Seasonable Hints from an Honest Man* (London, 1761), p. 37.

86.   *Junius*, pp. 152, 231.

87.   *Parliamentary History, 21*, 1290; *An Inquiry into the Origin and Consequences of the Influence of the Crown over Parliament* (London, 1780), pp. 36–7; *Thoughts on a Reform in the Representation of the People* (London, 1783), p. 10.

88.   Guttridge, *English Whiggism*, p. 118. For a searching analysis of royal influence see Archibald S. Foord, "The Waning of 'The Influence of the Crown'," *English Historical Review* (1947), *62*, 484-507.

89.   *Parliamentary History, 21*, 355.

90.   Barnes, *George III and William Pitt*, p. 14.

91.   *The True State of the Question*, pp. 13-14.

92.   *Thoughts on a Reform in the Representation of the People*, p. 10.

93.   D. L. Keir, "Economical Reform, 1779-1787," *Law Quarterly Review* (1934), *50*, 368-9.

94.   *Memoirs of George II, 2*, 204-5, given here in full from photostats of the manuscript which are in the possession of W. S. Lewis. Lord Holland's deletions are printed by Sedgwick in *From Anne to Victoria*, ed. Dobrée, p. 271.

95.   *Memoirs of George II, 1*, 136n; Walpole's *Reminiscences*, p. 84.

96.   *Memoirs of George III, 2*, 97.

97.   Pinkerton, *Walpoliana, 1*, 64.

98.   *Glenbervie Diaries, 2*, 98.

99.   James Earl Waldegrave, *Memoirs* (Philadelphia, 1822), p. 85; George III to Bute, [July 1], 1756, in *Letters from George III to Lord Bute*, ed. Sedgwick, pp. 2-3.

100.   George Nobbe, *The North Briton, A Study in Political Propaganda* (New York, 1939), pp. 44-5.

101.   *Memoirs of George III, 1*, 191; *Junius*, pp. 152-3.

102.   *A Catalogue of Prints and Drawings in the British Museum*, ed. F. C. Stephens (London, 1883), *4*, pp. lxxv-lxxix; *Memoirs of George III, 1* 263; Lecky, *History of England in the Eighteenth Century, 3*, 216.

103. *An Inquiry into the Origin and Consequences of the Influence of the Crown over Parliament*, p. 26.

104. *The Vicar of Wakefield* (1766), ch. 19; Feiling, *Second Tory Party*, p. 82.

105. Douglas, *Seasonable Hints from an Honest Man*, pp. 11, 61.

106. Catherine Macaulay [Graham], *Observations on . . . Thoughts on the Cause of the Present Discontents* (London, 1770), p. 7.

107. *Selections from the Letters and Correspondence of Sir James Bland Burges, Bart.*, ed. James Hutton (London, 1885), p. 64.

108. *The Farington Diary, ed.* James Greig (2nd ed., London, 1922), *1*, 139.

109. Butterfield, *George III and the Historians*, pp. 43, 61, 105, 138.

110. *Letters from George III to Lord Bute*, ed. Sedgwick, pp. xxiv-xl, lvi.

111. Namier, *England*, pp. 94-5.

112. Feiling, *Second Tory Party*, p. 5; Yorke, *Life of Hardwicke*, *1*, 383.

113. *Letters from George III to Lord Bute*, ed. Sedgwick, pp. xvii-xviii.

114. "The Conduct of the Allies" in Swift's *Works*, ed. Scott, *4*, 353; "A Dissertation upon Parties" in Bolingbroke's *Works* (Dublin, 1793), *2*, 8.

115. *Letters from George III to Lord Bute*, ed. Sedgwick, pp. xvii-xviii.

116. *Ibid.*; Bute to Lowther, November 17, 1762, quoted in Feiling, *Second Tory Party*, p. 69; Bute to Bedford, April 2, 1763, *Bedford Correspondence*, *3*, 224.

117. Butterfield, *George III and the Historians*, pp. 183, 233.

118. *Parliamentary History*, *23*, 559, 681, 852.

119. *Annual Register* (1778), *21*, 252-7; Elliot's diary in *Bedford Correspondence*, *3*, 284; *Parliamentary History*, *23*, 670-1, and *24*, 224.

120. Feiling, *Second Tory Party*, p. 102; *Letters from George III to Lord Bute*, ed. Sedgwick, pp. lxvi-lxviii; *Glenbervie Diaries*,

1, 284-5, 415; *Bedford Correspondence, 3*, p. xxxiii; *Croker Papers*, ed. L. J. Jennings (London, 1885), *3*, 179-80.

121. Trevor Williams, "The Cabinet in the Eighteenth Century," *History* (1938), *22*, 248; Namier, *England*, p. 183.

122. N. H. Fieldhouse, "Bolingbroke and the Idea of Non-Party Government," *History* (1939), *23*, 56 n. 2; Edward R. Turner, *The Cabinet Council of England* (London, 1930), *1*, 242-5.

123. Namier, *England*, p. 128; Feiling, *Second Tory Party*, p. 5; Waldegrave, *Memoirs*, pp. 104-5; Godolphin to Harley, March 22, 1705/6, in Historical MSS. Commission, *Portland MSS., 4*, 291.

124. Stanhope, *History of England, 5*, 116.

125. Sir Lewis Namier, *Conflicts, Studies in Contemporary History* (London, 1942), pp. 198-9. Butterfield objects to identifying the King's friends with civil servants (*George III and the Historians*, pp. 294-5).

126. Feiling, *Second Tory Party*, p. 100.

127. Hervey's *Memoirs*, ed. Sedgwick, *1*, p. liv.

128. *Letters from George III to Lord Bute*, ed. Sedgwick, p. lvi; Namier, *England*, pp. 94-5; Becker in *American Historical Review* (1911), *16*, 255; Feiling, *Second Tory Party*, p. 5; Guttridge, *English Whiggism*, p. 17; Barnes, *George III and William Pitt*, p. 7.

129. Wraxall's *Memoirs, 1*, 295.

130. George III to North, September 10, 1775, quoted in Guttridge, *English Whiggism*, p. 105.

131. *Ibid.*, p. 62.

132. Feiling, *Second Tory Party*, p. 103.

133. Rigby to Lord Spencer, March 26, 1770, quoted in *ibid.*; for his public remarks see *Parliamentary History, 23*, 598. See also Foord in *English Historical Review* (1947), *62*, 484.

134. Boswell's *Johnson*, Hill-Powell edn., *2*, 118.

135. Holdsworth, *History of English Law, 10*, 720; see also Fieldhouse in *History* (1939), *23*, 52.

136. Barnes, *George III and William Pitt*, p. 14; Guttridge, *English Whiggism*, pp. 32-3; see also Wraxall's *Memoirs, 2*, 286.

137. Trevelyan, *Early History of Charles James Fox*, p. 156.

138. *Memoirs of George III, 1,* 70, *3,* 243, and *4,* 203; Wraxall's *Memoirs, 2,* 83, 133, and *5,* 183.

139. Namier, *England,* p. 63; cf. Butterfield, *George III and the Historians,* p. 260.

140. *Ibid.,* pp. 259-60.

141. *Memoirs of George III, 2,* 97.

142. *Letters from George III to Lord Bute,* ed. Sedgwick, p. lvi.

143. Sedgwick in *From Anne to Victoria,* ed. Dobrée, pp. 276-7.

144. *Glenbervie Diaries, 2,* 9-10.

145. Ernst Cassirer, *The Myth of State* (New Haven, 1946), pp. 15, 37, 43, 47-8.

146. Max Radin, "Tradition," *Encyclopedia of the Social Sciences* (New York, 1935), *15,* 63.

147. *Memoirs of George III, 3,* 124-5; *Last Journals, 1,* 73.

148. Guttridge, *English Whiggism,* pp. 104-5.

149. See Bancroft's *History of the United States, 4,* 162, 245.

150. Unless otherwise indicated, materials for this paragraph are from Butterfield, *George III and the Historians,* pp. 61, 89-91, 104, 151, 155, 159-66, 176-80.

151. *Letters from George III to Lord Bute,* ed. Sedgwick, pp. xxxvii-xxxviii.

152. Herbert Butterfield, *The Whig Interpretation of History* (London, 1931), pp. 11-12.

153. *Letters from George III to Lord Bute,* ed. Sedgwick, pp. viii, xvi.

154. Feiling, *Second Tory Party,* pp. 3-5; Williams in *History* (1938), *22,* 241-2.

155. Namier, *England,* p. 94; see also pp. 58, 63, 179.

156. William Edwards, *Crown, People, and Parliament 1760-1935* (Bristol, 1937), p. 26. For a selection of similar statements about the constitutional significance of George III's reign, see Barnes, *George III and William Pitt,* pp. 493-504.

157. Butterfield, *George III and the Historians,* pp. 97, 108, 152, 165, 178.

158. Sedgwick in *From Anne to Victoria,* ed. Dobrée, p. 278.

159. Butterfield, *George III and the Historians,* pp. 108-9.

INDEX

117